SKYE REMEMBERED

Written and Compiled

by

DEREK COOPER

A' Ghaidhlig le MARTAINN DOMHNALLACH

ISBN 0 9508790 0 2

Published by the West Highland Publishing Company Limited
Old School, Breakish
Isle of Skye

Printed by Nevisprint Limited
Claggan Road
Fort William

Contents

LIST OF PHOTOGRAPHS

Foreword

Owning a camera was far beyond the means of most people on Skye until after the Great War when the Kodak 'Brownie' made all of us into potential 3/6d George Washington Wilsons. Up to then it was the rich who had pointed cameras at themselves and at the poor. Pictures in those days were carefully posed; if you moved you became a blur. So there is an artificiality present. Peasants seen cutting peats or holding a cas chrom have been told what to do. It looks that way because that's the way it was.

But at that very time, in the politically active 1880s, the ordinary people on Skye were beginning to realise that their rights were worth fighting for. No photographs of the Battle of the Braes, alas. In those days newspapers published line drawings, artists' impressions of what happened, not the vivid actuality of the reporter with the Leica. All these pictures make their own social comment; the text, I hope, puts the images in context.

I am most grateful to everyone who sent me photographs, helped me find them or who supplied vital information to identify them. Although my own first-hand memories of Skye begin around the late 1920s I have been able to call on a number of friends with a remarkable knowledge of the island going back much further than that.

To everyone who entered into the spirit of the hunt my thanks and if I have inadvertently missed out any names my apologies. Particularly helpful were Ian Campbell, Alexander Fenton, Mr and Mrs Donald Fraser, Mrs Evelyn Macdonald, Lord Godfrey Macdonald, Jonathan Macdonald, Martin Macdonald, Duncan MacInnes, Donnie Mackenzie, Ewen Mackenzie, John Mackenzie, Alan Mackinnon, Charles John Mackinnon, Donald Maclean, Will Maclean, Jeff Macleod, Dr Jim Mitchell, Donnie Munro, Iain Noble, Rob Macdonald Parker, David Scott, Mrs Evelyn Stockwell, Dr David Roberts, George Taylor, Roger Taylor, Sine Threlfall and Mr and Mrs Mark Wathen.

To Roger Hutchinson, midwife of this venture, Norrie Matheson who designed the layout and Caroline MacKechnie who set the words a big thank you. I owe a special debt to Brian Wilson without whose persistence and vision there would have been no West Highland Publishing Company. This is the first book they have published; I hope there will be many more.

Derek Cooper
Portree
January, 1983.

An t-Eilean

An e fearas-mhor a tha a' toirt air na Sgitheanaich an dachaidh ainmeachadh mar sin, mar nach robh eilean eile air clar an t-saoghail ach e fhein? Neo direach uaisleachd nadurra as an aite 'sna thogadh iad? Neo gu dearbh tuiteamas eachdraidh canain, agus gum bheil e nas fhasa da fhacal a chleachdadh an aite tri? Bidh sinn coir dhuinn fhein, is canaidh sinn gur e measgachadh de uaisleachd nadurra is tuiteamas a th'ann!

Ach leis an fhirinn is docha gum bheil tri eileanan air am filleadh anns an aon seo — Trondairnis mu thuath, Duthaich MhicLeoid mu'n iar, agus Srath MhicFhionghuin is Sleibhte mu dheas. "Mo chuideachd fhein coin Throndairnis!" ars an t-seann bhosd, agus is iongantach cho beag comunn 's a th'ann fhathast eadar coin Throndairnis is faochagan an t-Sratha. B'ann ri Uibhist a bha ceanglaichean Throndairnis, ris na Hearadh ceanglaichean Dhuthaich MhicLeoid agus ri Loch Aillse is Ceann t-Saile a bha an ceann a deas ag coimhead. Fiu's an diugh chan eil lorgan nan seann dilseachd sin air an dubhadh as.

Ach cha robh an saoghal amuigh a' faicinn ach aon eilean, is An Cuilthionn ag eirigh os a chionn is 'ga cheangal ri cheile; bho'n taobh astigh bhathas a' faicinn na dearbh bheanntan mar sgaradh, ged a b'fhiach iad bosd neo dha gun teagamh nuair a thigeadh e gu bearradaireachd ri eileanaich eile.

Lorg an saoghal a muigh an t-Eilean Sgitheanach trath. Sgap Dr Johnston is Sir Walter Scott is ioma sgriobhadair eile 'san naoidheamh linn deug aon seorsa eolais air. Gle thric b'e an seorsa eolais a bha tuilleadh is cus an comain rannghal gun bhrigh mu'n Phrionnsa Tearlach 's a chuid siubhail neo sithichean a' dannsa air barr an fhraoich.

Ach bha eolas na b'fhirinniche 's na bu chruaidhe na sin ri lorg air. Bithear an dochas gun nochd pairt dhe a dealbhan an leabhair seo.

Frontispiece. **On the ramparts of Dunvegan which claims to be the oldest inhabited castle in Britain a nineteenth century Macleod descended from the thirteenth century clan founder Leod poses for posterity. Cumbersome equipment, tripod essential, this is the kind of plate camera which took most of the pictures in this book.**

The World of Work

"The climate is surpassingly changeable, very moist and not a little severe," wrote a correspondent in Skye in 1844, "Scarcely one day in four throughout the year is free from rain, still less from clouds; the varieties of frost, thaw, snow, rain, storm and calm are often experienced in a day: snow sometimes lies from three to seven weeks and may occasionally be seen on the highest ground in the middle of June: winds prevail in August or September so tempestuous as frequently to demolish the expectations of the husbandman; and suddenly amassed clouds sometimes burst asunder on the mountains and pour down their contents in impetuous and thundering torrents which deluge the plains below and render the merest ordinary rill impassable." Allowing for a slight hyperbole, that's not a bad description of what it was like, and is like, to be a farmer in Skye.

It was against this background that peats were cut, crops sown, animals raised and toil undertaken. There were too many mouths to feed from the small quantities of land that the people possessed. When a particularly bad summer caused a failure of the crops many became destitute. No one had savings to fall back on.

When Robert Somers visited Skye after the potato famine of 1846 he found a dispiriting scene: "Every object wears the desolate aspect of a place deserted by the hand of industry. Land unploughed and unenclosed; houses bare, dilapidated and unapproached by roads or foot-paths. The agriculture of Skye is more indeed like the puny scratchings of savages than the powerful agriculture of civilised life."

Everything seemed to conspire against the industrious and it is small wonder that vast numbers in the nineteenth century accepted assisted passages overseas. For the majority life was uncouth and uncomfortable. Debarred from the land they existed as best they could. "There are on our township," a crofter told the Napier Commission in 1882, "double the number of tenants that I have seen upon it and the hill pasture was taken from us. We were ordered not to keep a single sheep. We were for several years without sheep after which the proprietor gave us liberty to keep five or six. The few we have now are spoiling our township for want of pasture. Many of us have no better bed-clothes than old bags, formerly used in conveying whelks to Glasgow. Sometimes when a poor man gets a good meal-bag he converts it into underclothing."

Another brave voice: "We were next forbidden to keep horses and had to do their work by carrying burdens on our backs. During the last year I have put on my land 200 creels of sea-weed all of which I have had to carry myself. In ascending from the shore to our township the braes is so steep that we have to hold on by our hands."

It was a self-perpetuating treadmill of misery from which the only escape was emigration or death. And yet there was music and song and a strong capacity for survival.

There were indeed those, like the episcopal rector in Portree, who saw the crofter's lot as an ennobling one. Writing in 1907 he cautioned visitors not to be too upset if they saw scanty patches of land being tended in the pouring rain: "The crofter is contented with it; he is not overdriven with work; the work is congenial; he is a son of the soil; he can turn to many other occupations; and compared with the lot of slum-dwellers in towns his is a pleasant one.

"How few men can say what is true of the crofter so long as he pays his rent and observes the rules of his township, that he is independent and his own master? Besides this he is pursuing a business which somehow seems to be bound up with the truer life of man. Nature and he understand each other; from her he learns many virtues; his ambitions are few and easily attained. Happy crofter who knows nothing of *sturm and drang* and has enough to live on of simple food and has learned contentment apart from ease and luxury."

Teachd-an-tir is Cosnadh

Dha'n chroitear 's dha'n choitear 'san naoidheamh linn deug bha an teachd-an-tir cugallach; air a chuingleachadh le cion fearainn, droch uachdarain is droch shide. A' bhliadhna a lobhadh am buntata agus a bhiodh an corca gorm is tana 'san achadh aig deireadh an fhoghair, neo 'na laighe ag grodadh fo chuideam an uisge, cha bhiodh ann dhaibh ach maorach a' chladaich is uidhean fhaoileag. Air cho truagh 's gun robh iad bhiodh geola aig cuideigin 'sa bhaile, agus latha amach dha na h-eileanan beaga — Fladaigh Chuain neo An t-Iasgair neo Ascraib, can — is gheibhte de dh'uidhean eoin-mhara a dheanadh diadhaid neo dha dha'n teaghlach le beagan a bharrachd a reicte dha'n mharsanta air annlan. Agus air cho truagh 's gun robh cuisean bha an comhnaidh marsanta beag anns gach baile. Treubh righinn, na marsantan.

Is docha gun robh an lon beagan na bu chinntiche do luchd-obrach an tighe mhoir is nan tuathanach is nam fear-tac. Saorsa na croite — saorsa na bochdainn, gle thric, 'sna h-amannan ud — 'ga reic air beagan not le cinnt 'san leth-bhliadhna, cabair an uachdarain mu dhruim an teaghlaich, feurachd mart bainne is laogh agus corra pheat uain mur an robh an corr aite ann dha. Na greidhearan 's na ciobairean 's na sgalagan; nighean dubh a' chidsin is na h-ighneagan a bhiodh mu'n chro feasgar (bha meas aig na baird orra) 's fhathast a' suidheachadh a' bhainne mu mheadhon-oidhche is air an gluinean a' lasadh nan teinntean a rithist mu shia 'sa mhadainn. Bhiodh latha dheth aca 'sa chola-deug, is docha, is rachadh iad dhachaidh gu'n teaghlaichean le sgilling neo dha ma bha iad fortanach. Fhuair na greidhearan is na ciobairean gu h-araid droch laimhseachadh aig am an Land League; "an duine tha leis an uachdaran chan eil e leinne," chanadh am braithrean riutha.

Ach, gun teagamh, cha robh na criochan buileach dubh is geal mar sin. Ged a b'ann o shliochd chroitear, choiteir neo ghreidheir thu — neo bho cholmadh dhiubh air fad — ma dh'fhaoidte, air chor air choireigin, gun togadh tu ciaoird. Cha robh an t-Eilean Sgitheanach idir gun shaoir, gun charpantairean, gun chlachairean, gun mhuillearan anns an linn a tha direach bhuainn. Bha an taillear a' seodal o thigh gu tigh ag iarraidh bord fo thoin, briogais fo shnathad, biadh 'na bhroinn agus fear-tighe a dh'eisdeadh ri sgeulachdan fad seachdain; agus, nuair a dh'fhalbhadh e, an tasdan geal 'na dhorn.

Agus an comhnaidh bha an imrich ann. Cha b'e imrich cuain idir (ged nach robh sin 'na annas) ach imrich cosnaidh, le lan duil gun tilleadh tu. Uair a thilleadh is uair nach tilleadh. Eil fhios cia-meud a chaidh fodha le deoch an cuiltean Ghlaschu, le iomhaigh bhriste dhe'n Chuilthionn air cul an inntinn? Agus an fheadhainn eile rinn spaidsearachd air urlair a' Ghlasgow Skye le

eileadh ur is sporan lan, agus iomhaigh fhann dhe'n Chuilthionn gu comhfhurtail air cul an inntinn?

Ach bha cuid a thill; a thug am beo-shlaint a Galldachd (Galldachd Alba is galldachd an t-saoghail) 's a thill. Fear dhiubh Lachlainn Mor MacLeoid as a' Chamus-mhor an Cille-mhoire, a thug seachd bliadhna air bruaichean Chluaidh ann an 80an na linn a dh'fhalbh gun a theaghlach fhaicinn 'san uine sin; ach a chum beo iad 's a thill dhachaidh an ceann nan seachd bliadhna.

"Bha fhios againn gun robh e beo," thuirt Ceat Lachlainn Mhoir, a bhiodh eadar na sia 's na tri deug a dh'aois aig an am. "Cha robh sgriobhadh aige ach bhiodh bolla mine a' tighinn bhuaithe a dh'Uige air an Dunara a h-uile mios."

Thug Murchadh a bhrathair, na b'fhaide a' tilleadh; fichead bliadhna (neo an e deich bliadhna air fhichead?) air a' pholas ann an Hong Kong. Dh'fhan Uilleam, an treabhaiche, aig baile, ach an t-seachdain neo dha a thug e anns a' Chalton Gaol an Dun-eidinn son suil air fhiaradh a thoirt air polasmain Ivory nuair a bha stri a' Land League aig a h-airde.

"Bha sianar bhraithrean an teaghlach m'athair," chanadh Ceat Lachlainn Mhoir, "a h-uile duine dhiubh os cionn sia troighean a dh'airde!"

Agus bha moran dhiubh mar sin, fir is mnathan, a chleachd an cosnadh gus an fheadhainn aig an tigh a chuideachadh le'n teachd-an-tir. Na h-iasgairean, air bataichean chaich air cladaichean Eirinn, neo an Inbhir-uige neo 'sa Bhruaich; ach dhachaidh aig am cur an t-sil is am cur na sguaib dha'n adaig nam b'urrainn dhaibh idir. Na "navvies" a' togail loighne a' reile eadar Glaschu is An Gearasdan is Malaig; is ameasg an seorsa fhein — ge b'e Eireannaich neo Goill — a cur uisge troimh phiob gu factraidh British Aluminium an Ceann-loch-liobhainn.

Ceat Lachlainn Mhoir is a seorsa a' falbh bliadhna neo dha air shearbhantas gu tighean mora Hillhead; bliadhna neo dha gus achaidhean arbhair a lomadh do thuathanaich an Eilein Duibh. Fichead bliadhna roimhe sin Mor Eoghainn Alasdair Eoghainn is a comh-aoisean a'falbh le'n corrain gu machraichean Labhdaidh, far nach tuigeadh iad Gaidhlig, mar a dheanadh muinntir an Eilein Duibh ged bu mhor leotha aideachadh 's a bruidheann.

Domhnall Alasdair Ruairidh — ged a tha e an diugh 'san uaigh chan eil deich bliadhna fichead bho'n sguir e dhe'n fhasan seo — a bhith cur an t-sil 's a' bhuntata as t-earrach, a bhith a' togail air gu cosnadh ameasg an Skye Navy air a' Queen Mary II air Cluaidh fad an t-samhraidh, 's a bhith aig baile nuair a bhiodh na cruachan 'gan cur dha'n iodhlann.

Daoine a ghleidh am muinntir fhein.

Photographers were few and far between. If one called you put on your best Sabbath dress with a suitable bonnet and brought your 'Saxony' spinning wheel out of the peat-smoke darkness. The wheel was turned by a treadle and the machine was designed to wind and twist at the same time.

Dyeing the wool. The most common colour in the Hebrides was a soft reddish-brown, imparted by a coarse rock lichen or *crotal*. Bog myrtle yielded a rich yellow; heather gathered just before it came into flower, a dark green; the elder in combination with alum produced a profound blue. The bark of the root of yellow lady's-bedstraw provided a rich red, and heather in flower was a source of clear yellow. Peat soot would be boiled in a bag to furnish a yellowish-brown colour. The wool and the plants and roots which would yield the desired colour were put into an iron pot and boiled. Here a hank of wool is being lifted out with a stick to see whether the right shade of colour has been reached. The yarn would often be left to steep in pots of different dyes and afterwards the hanks were hung up to dry. As with making scones some women were skilled at dyeing, others just didn't have the knack and produced dull and muddy colours. The beauty of these vegetable dyes was that the colours stayed fast and never faded. It is a skill known now only to those with Art College Diplomas.

At the wooden loom. Weaving was traditionally a woman's task. It was women too who waulked the cloth after it had been woven. Waulking or fulling to shrink cloth was hard work. The cloth was first soaked in urine diluted with hot water then wrung out and spread in a U-shape on the waulking table. The women of the township summoned by the goodwife of the house then began to beat and rub the cloth passing it down the table. It was a rhythmical exercise and from the rhythm there grew waulking songs. Working the heavy wet cloth called for slow and solemn songs then as the cloth dried and became lighter the songs too grew quicker and jollier. In earlier days the women sat on the ground in two rows feet to feet with the cloth between them working it with their bare toes. "Their song", as Mrs Gordon Cumming recorded in the 1880s "growing louder and louder as they warm to their work, so that a casual observer is extremely apt to imagine that he has suddenly stumbled on the inmates of some private lunatic asylum".

Left. Milking the cows. Women were the backbone and mainstay of the family. They fetched and carried, looked after the animals, cooked, sewed, spun, and wove, made butter and crowdie, bore the children, made the clothes and in the heyday of illicit distillation made the whisky too. And they still found the time to sing.

Right. Macleod of Macleod built many mills in Skye. They were a useful source of income. Small domestic querns were often outlawed thus forcing the tenants to bring their corn to the laird's mill to be ground.

Far Right. John Mackenzie, the most famous mountain guide in Scottish history died in 1933 after 50 years of climbing in the Cuillins. He was with the Pilkington brothers when they made the first ascent of the Inaccessible Pinnacle and was the first to set foot on A' Cioch in Corrie Lagan. Born in 1856 in a croft at Sconser he climbed Sgurr nan Gillean at the age of ten. By the end of his life he had probably ascended to the Cuillin peaks on a thousand separate occasions. There are many stories told about him. In 1895 a party came back to Sligachan Inn and told John that they had climbed the Inaccessible Peak by the steep western route. Impossible, said John. Excuse us they said, but we did! "I don't doubt your word", said John, "I *know* it's impossible; I've been up it ma'sel". His old friend Professor Norman Collie who lies buried beside him in Struan cemetery wrote: "He is the only real British Climbing Guide that has ever existed. Neither the Lake District nor North Wales has produced one. As a companion on a long summer day he was perfect. Always cheerful, keenly alive to everything — the wild birds, the deer on the hillside, the fish in the rivers and all the natural things. There is no one who can take his place. Those who know him will remember him as a perfect gentleman who never offended by word or deed".

The miller at the Hinnisdal mill.

John Mackenzie: "the courtesy joined to self-respect that are the heritage of the clans" — Sheriff Valentine.

Where there were no piers, as at Staffin and Kilmaluag, boats would row out to the steamer and bring back the baskets of bread and supplies from Glasgow landing them on the beach. This is Armadale before the deep water pier was built.

Sligachan, the most famous climbing inn in Britain. The first recorded ascent was by the Rev C Lesingham Smith in 1835. From that time onwards, the inn was used by all the Cuillin pioneers — Sheriff Nicolson, Professors James Forbes and Norman Collie and the Pilkington brothers.

Kyleakin hotel and staff. "A pleasant resting-place for the tourist and especially the artist, possessing as it does some of the finest views in the Western Highlands. Ben-na-Cailleach 2,387 feet high, rises behind it". — Contemporary Guide.

Puffer. With a skipper, an engineer, a mate and a deckhand these small steam ships were economical to run. They were used for carrying coal, stone, sand, building materials, fencing, salt, corrugated iron, barbed wire and the hardware of a community. Their flat bottoms enabled them to sit foursquare on the seabed at low tide when a procession of horses and carts would help with the unloading. If unloading wasn't completed in one ebb the puffer would ride at anchor until the next low tide. The average puffer was about 65 feet long and could take 100 tons of coal which would be unloaded by a derrick mounted on the mast. Puffers chugged round the islands at six knots, the successors to the eighteenth century sailing smacks. A puffer used to bring barley to Talisker distillery at Carbost on the shores of Loch Harport and take away the full casks of whisky. Modern puffers are diesel; but the lorry has almost made them redundant.

Crofter and his wife, Sleat.

"Since a small croft of itself cannot support a family, the crofter or his son must perforce employ their energies in supplementing their crofting work by other employments. Thus they are compelled to go fishing; some of them find lucrative wages as yachtsmen during the season; others go as navvies or get the occasional occupation in large towns. His potato crop makes a staple article of diet for himself and his family all the year round. His wife can always obtain a price for her fowls and eggs. Family affection is very strong among the crofters and the croft always offers a home for daughters who are in service or sons employed in Glasgow when they have a holiday. They know that they are always welcome there and that the homestead will never be wanting to them. As you pass through the township, quiet Celtic faces gaze at you or politely wish you "good-day". It may not be a very animated scene but it has its own suggestion of quiet life and work, of industry after nature's heart. You are among people who depend almost entirely on old mother-earth for food and fuel. And all around the peaceful township stretches the silent moor to the distant hills or the blue sea". *The Misty Isle of Skye* by the misty-eyed Rev J A Macculloch, the former rector of St Columba's, Portree.

Domhnall na Coille, the postman. Appointed just before the Great War, Donald the Post delivered the Royal Mail on foot to the townships of Glenmore. William Mackenzie in his memoirs published in 1930 recalled a postman who used to carry the mail from Portree to Kilmuir three times a week. "Old Iain Posta (as his father Donnchadh Posta before him) did the double journey forty miles each day and his bag did not inconvenience him. There was no service to Staffin. An old woman crossed the moor to Kilmuir once a week and, wrapped in a red handkerchief, brought back what letters there were which she distributed receiving twopence each."

The Minister and his wife, Waternish. Note the wretched state of the unmetalled road compared with the smart turn out of the trap and its owner. "I daresay", wrote Malcolm Ferguson in 1899, "there is no district of equal extent and population in all Skye which is less known generally than Waternish. It is in a manner isolated from any of the highways throughout the island and reached only by a primitive cart road which has to be retraced on leaving it, it is so far hid by surrounding hills from almost any part of the island, except from the sea sailing up Loch Dunvegan or crossing Loch Bay."

A party from Penifiler collecting seaweed on the Scorribreac shore of Portree bay in the 1880s. The collecting and carrying of seaweed to ameliorate the land was regarded as work for women and girls. Potatoes, oats, rye and mixed corn would be the main crops.

Cattle grazing outside Portree where the cattle market was held every May. Farmers, cattle dealers, drovers and now and again "show folks" and peddlers would all gather. "Straight before us was a wide, circular sloping heath and heather-clad valley, dotted all over for miles on either side of the road, and all in commotion, with people and lowing, bellowing cattle and dogs, slowly advancing from all the airts of the compass towards the market stance". *Calum Macfhearghais.*

Cutting peats in Trotternish.

Peat cutting began towards the end of April and the whole family would join in. Like shearing, going to the peatbanks was very much a communal activity. In the days before puffers began to bring in coal from Ardrossan townships were entirely dependent for warmth and cooking fuel on peat. It has been estimated that an average family burnt 18,000 peats a year; one thousand peats could be cut by one man in a day. They were piled up to dry before being taken later in the year, usually by cart, to be stacked beside the croft house. Lying in the moor the peat is over 90 per cent water. It was peat which limited the inventiveness of the Skye diet. Used as a fuel very little beyond boiling and simmering could be accomplished. Mutton, herring, potatoes and whatever root vegetables were grown would be boiled and any baking would be done in the hot ashes of the fire.

A horse and cart in Staffin in the days before the car. "It has been alleged that the crofter is a lazy, easy-going person. Nothing could be farther from the truth; the average crofter has a life of unremitting toil. As his is an open-air life, there must be periods of enforced idleness and these have to be overcome by additional effort. There is no question of a seven or eight hour day in his vocation or is there any ca' canny. His hours are from dawn to dusk. His labour begins in early spring — delving, sowing, planting, harrowing take up his time; peat-cutting, fitting, stacking, and carrying home absorb a part. Weeding, hoeing, sheep shearing and dipping, tending cattle etc., bring him to harvesting of oats and potatoes. His stacks and houses have to be made secure from winter gales. His sole relaxation is a change of labour. Housing, feeding and tending cattle keep him fully employed during the short winter days. The alleged laziness is by persons utterly ignorant of the crofter and crofter life. Where the family circumstances permit he may engage in seasonal employment away from home. His surroundings, pure open air and the purest of water invigorate his nerves". William Mackenzie *Skye: Iochdar-Trotternish*.

Cas chrom — the wooden hand plough particularly useful on stony ground and essential for the majority of crofters who lacked either the money or the grazing to keep horses. "A great part of the land instead of being ploughed by cattle is cultivated with human labour and dug by an instrument called the Cascrome, in English the crooked foot, or crooked spade. This is a strong coarse spade about six feet long with a thick flat wooden head armed at the extremity with a sharp narrow piece of iron. The great length of the shaft and the bulky wooden head which serves as a fulcrum form a lever of considerable power. This instrument is exceedingly well adapted to cultivate the earth among fixed rocks, where the plough cannot go or where the soil is so filled with large loose stones as not to be arable. With this instrument a Highlander will open up more ground in a day and render it fit for the sowing of grain, than could be done by two or three men with any other spades that are commonly used. If he works assiduously from about Christmas to near the end of April he will prepare land sufficient to sow five bolls.* In the course of the season he will cultivate as much land with his spade as is sufficient to supply a family of seven or eight persons, the year round, with meal and potatoes." *An Economical History of the Hebrides.* John Walker. 1808.

* One boll equals 140 pounds.

Toil was unremitting and the rewards never rose above subsistence level. In a bad summer when the peats failed to dry out, the hay lay in the wet in the fields and the corn never ripened, destitution and famine were never far away.

Oxcart in Trotternish.

James Munro outside Macfarlane the butcher's in Wentworth Street, Portree 1933. He and his mare Mollie delivered milk round the town from the home farm twice a day seven days a week.

The shearing. The traditional Skye date to start shearing was June 15th. All the crofters of a township would handle their sheep at a common fank and the occasion was then, as it still is, as social as it was essential.

Harvesting the corn Gesto 1891. The photograph was taken by Jessie Scott, daughter of John Scott, tacksman of Drynoch from 1848 to 1896. In a memoir Scott wrote, "the casual labour all came from the crofting township of Coillore, a miserable collection of thatched hovels with in some cases the animals sharing them. In those days a shepherd had a house, £20 a year, the right to keep two cows and 6½ bolls of meal. The daily rate for casual labour was 1/6d for a man 9d for a woman." The Drynoch accounts for the years between 1867 and 1888 reveal an average yearly profit of £1062. In that period the total annual wages paid was less than £200.

The Encircling Sea

Until 1830 it took up to fifteen days to get from Skye to Glasgow under sail. It is not surprising that large numbers of people never left the island at all. Then in 1830 David Hutcheson & Company inaugurated a weekly steamer service to the south and thus began the island's long love-hate affair with the steamship companies.

David MacBrayne was a partner in Hutcheson and in 1879 he began to carry on business under his own name. It was not long before a wag had produced a quatrain to celebrate the relationship:

The earth belongs unto the Lord
And all that it contains
Except the Western Highlands
And they are all MacBrayne's!

The islanders were completely dependent on MacBrayne for both passenger and cargo transport. Cattle and sheep were taken to the mainland by MacBrayne; when there was a war the volunteers left by MacBrayne, and those who survived came back by MacBrayne. It was a MacBrayne steamer which took the arrested crofters to the mainland at the time of the Battle of the Braes.

It was on a MacBrayne steamer, the *Clansman*, that Alexander Smith left Skye on his last voyage south to Edinburgh before writing *A Summer in Skye*.

"The *Clansman* reached Portree Bay at eleven p.m. and I went on board at once and went to bed. When I awoke next morning the engines were in full action and I could hear the rush of water past my berth. When I got on deck we were steaming down the Sound of Raasay. A lot of sheep were penned up near the bows, amidships were piles of wool, groups of pointers and setters were scattered about and at the breakfast table were numerous sportsmen returning to the south, whose conversation ran on grouse-shooting, salmon-fishing and deer-stalking."

The arrival of the steamer at the pier of a small township was the signal for everyone to gather and exchange the latest gossip. The steamer and her crew were carriers of both cargo and news; for many isolated communities it was their only contact with the outside world.

When journalist Ian Anderson arrived at the pier in Loch Pooltiel on board the *Hebrides* he felt as if he had suddenly entered into the centre of a village "social". This was about eighty years ago; the boat was late and didn't arrive until it was dark: "At the corner of the pier stood the Pier Master swinging his oil lantern for the ship's guidance to assist it in berthing. The open-fronted shed on the pier was filled with people from all parts of the surrounding district and all actively engaged in conversation under the feeble yellow rays of the oil lamp illuminating the shed. This was seemingly an event and it appeared that all came to the pier whether for goods or not. The pier was the meeting place for this outlying community. No sooner was the cargo unloaded than the people began to drift away in twos or threes and as our last ropes were drawn on board, even the mast with the lamp had disappeared."

Nearly every able-bodied man on Skye with a boat or a place in a boat followed the fish. But it was a chancy business and when the herring shoals failed to appear in a loch then people went hungry. In 1787 the Scottish Fishery Society had established a fishing station at Stein but it failed to prosper. There were many reasons for this, not least the cost of salt needed for curing fish.

The people eked out the produce from their small patches of land by fishing for cod and ling. "It is observed," wrote Robert Somers, "that the crofters who fish diligently pay their rents with punctuality while those who are negligent in this respect are in arrears and in misery."

The seashore provided kelp and the kelp industry which prospered during the Napoleonic wars was responsible for a disastrous rise in the population. Ironically when there were too many mouths to feed, it was shellfish picked from the same shore that saved many a life.

Cuantan an Eilein

Chan eil eilean ann nach eil an cuan 'na phairt dheth. Agus bha e 'na phairt cho nadurrach de dhualchas an Sgitheanaich is nach robhas riamh 'ga ainmeachadh neo a smaoineachadh air mar rud-eigin air leth. Bha eolas cuain de sheorsa air choireigin mar tarraing analach.

Na Sgitheanaich bu mhotha dh'fhuiling taire cuain b'iad muinntir a' Ghlinne Mhoir, agus b'e taire nam bard a dh'fhuiling iadsan! Is ioma rann eibhinn a rinneadh a' moladh (ma b'fhior!) snas mara nan Gleannach. Bha an Gleann Mor ceithir mile bho'n mhuir, an aon bhaile a b'fhaide bho'n chladach 'san eilean. Ceithir mile, is bha thu air do mheas aineolach air gluasadan a' chuain!

Bha an cuan mar a bha an Cuilthionn, romhad 's as do dheidh ge b'e taobh a thionndaidheadh tu. Bha e moran na b'fheumaile na an Cuilthionn, ach a cheart cho gionach air beatha dhaoine. Is gann mile dhe'n chladach gun bron a' bhathaidh an crochadh ris uaireigin, gu h-araid 's 'san ochdamh 'san naoidheamh linn deug nuair a bha sruthan a' chost 'nan rathad-mor dha na h-eileanaich. Agus, is cinnteach, ioma linn riomhe sin bho'n bhuail a' cheud choite air cladach.

Ach bha cobhair 'sa chuan cuideachd; iasg is maorach a chumadh tomhas de bheo ri daoine breoite nuair a chaidh glasan nan uachdaran air fearann an sinnsreachd. Ach cladach cruaidh a bh'ann, cladach creagach gun traighean geala neo gainmheach mhin. ''Is uaibhreach creagan Ghearraidh, sailean os an cionn,'' ars Mairi Mhor nan Oran, is i fhein ag cur ris an uaibhreachas sin le ceol. Uaibhreach gun teagamh, ach de cho cunnartach? Ma bha sgeula a' bhathaidh cumanta troimh nan linntean, bha cuideachd is sgeulachd tuit gu bas air na creagan; balaich oga mar bu trice is iad air toir uighean e mhara.

B'e an cuan cuideachd an rathad-mor gu deas is gu'n t-saoghal mhor corr is ceud bliadhna. Bho latha a' *Ghlencoe* gu latha a' *Lochnevis* eil fhios meud de shliochd an eilein a ghabh an cursa triomh na caolais gu'n C is Malaig? Barrachd na rinn an turus air ais gu Loch Phort-ruigheadl neonach. Neo an turus eile air an *Dunara* bho Uige is Dun-bheagai Gleanndail deas gu Glaschu; oidhcheannan dorcha, stoirmeil glaiste fo is i a' stri ri cuantan borba mu Mhaol Chinn-tire. Ach na'n leigeadh an tin mara leat bha cothrom ann eolas a chur air cinnich annasach mar Leodhas is Hearaich is Uibhistich. Is ioma Sgitheanach a fhuair a cheud fhiosrach nach b'e ''an t-eilean'' an aon eilean a bh'ann air an dearbh bhata!

Tha latha nam bataichean sin seachad a nise. Chan ionnan ce mionaidean air aiseag a' Chaoil, is tu 'nad shuidhe aig a' chuibhle am fichead car eile, ri turus a' chost. Is gu'n ire sin tha an aiseag ghoiri lughdachadh ''eileanas'' an eilein. Gu dearbh — agus can fo t'anail e cluinn na Sgitheanaich thu — am bheil ann tuilleadh ach pairt de thir-r

Ach latha ri port le stoirm 'sa Chaol is gheibh thu am freagairt. Tha (Acainn thall a cheart cho fada bhuat ri Hiort. Tha an cuan fhathast 'na pl dhe'n eilean, cho cinnteach ris a' Chuilthionn.

The Waternish estate smack at Isay. The island was used for grazing cattle and sheep. On September 23, 1773 Macleod offered Isay to Dr Johnson ''on condition of his residing on it three months in the year. Mr Johnson was highly pleased with the fancy. He talked a great deal of his island — how he would build a house, how he would fortify it, how he would sally out and take the Isle of Muck; and then he laughed with a glee that was astonishing and could hardly leave off''. Boswell.

The paddle steamer *Glencoe* leaving Kyle for Portree in 1930. She was built in 1846 and became the Portree mail steamer at the end of the Great War. She carried a model of a golden eagle, over the dining saloon entrance and in the third class cabin a notice read: "This cabin has accommodation for 90 third-class passengers when not occupied by sheep, cattle, cargo or other encumbrances."

The 'Zulu' herring boats anchored in Portree Bay. "The signs of the arrival of the herrings are flocks of gulls who catch up the fish while they skim the surface and of the gannets who plunge and bring them up from considerable depths". Pennant.

Officers of the *Claymore*. With its handsome figurehead, yacht-like bow and well-proportioned lines the *Claymore* built in 1881 was probably the most elegant steamer ever ordered by David MacBrayne. She served in Hebridean waters for 50 years with only one serious mishap — a grounding on the rocks at the north end of Pabay in January 1910. Towed to Broadford by the *Sheila* she lay beached for a month; after extensive repairs she was back on station in July. *Claymore* was broken up in 1931.

A MacBrayne crew. The complement of a passenger steamer at the turn of the century was the skipper, 2 mates, a chief and second engineer, purser, 2 donkeymen, 2 firemen, a bosun, 2 winchmen, 6 crewmen, a chief steward, a cook and a pantry boy.

Fisherman. A man who in his day may well have rounded the Horn and crossed the South China seas. Many Skyemen found work on MacBrayne boats; others went further afield. In Victorian times there was plenty of employment to be had on the luxury steam yachts that cruised northern waters after the annual pleasures of Cowes. Lord Macdonald himself had one of the most beautiful yachts of all. ''When *The Lady of the Isles* came through the Sound of Raasay we watched her with pride as if she were our own. Ian Ban, who served in her for two seasons, would tell us how her captain, his own second cousin on his mother's side, told him that the bills for the cruise in the Mediterranean came to over £500 a month. And when Ian Ban described the dinner given by Lord Macdonald at Gibralter to the officers of the Cameron Highlanders and the wonderful wines of the country that they quaffed, we felt too as if we were partaking of royal banquets.

''In those golden days when Lord Macdonald brought his family from London to Skye, he came all the way by special train with his whole retinue of servants. At Strome Ferry *The Lady of the Isles* lay at the pier and soon the luggage was piled on board and the great company gathered on deck and the yacht sailed proudly through the Kyles to Armadale Castle. To the islanders it was a yearly feast of wonder''. *The Former Days* by Norman Maclean.

Claymore 760 tons, at Armadale Pier. The MacBrayne fleet was composed of cargo boats and fast steamers which carried both goods and passengers. In the summer months the deep-sea steamers were packed with visitors cruising Hebridean waters from Iona to St Kilda. You could have a week's sail among the Western Isles on the *Claymore* in the unruffled summer of 1899 for £4. ''Nowhere in all the world is there a holiday region of such endless and varied charm as that which lies among the Hebrides and nowhere is the means of travelling so easy, comfortable and altogether delightful. As the swift steamer with its gay company on board, sails through firths and narrows, sea-loch and sound, it is not only a panorama of scenic magnificence that the pilgrim sees pass by. The glories of green island and purple mountain indeed are there, with sun-swept glens and deep narrow inlets running far into recesses of the hills. Nowhere either, do sunset and evening star paint sea and shore and heaven with so splendid a pageantry. Then there are pleasant little towns where the steamer puts in for an hour or two, the clachan piers it touches at, to set a passenger or so ashore, and the island roadsteads where a boat comes out and is towed alongside for a few moments in the clear green seas, while the mails are taken on board. There is the plaintive sound of the Gaelic, the fragrance of the peat-reek drifting from the shore, and the bleat of the sheep far up the mountain-side that comes faintly to the ear.'' David MacBrayne Guide 1914. In those days MacBrayne had a fleet of twelve paddle steamers and 22 screw-driven steamers.

Cable Nook, Kyle of Lochalsh with the *Claymore* about to leave for Glasgow.

"Kyle of Lochalsh is built round its railway and harbour and these are the main supports of its population. When I first came to live there, it consisted of a miscellaneous collection of about eighty dwellings. Several were comfortable stone-walled buildings but others were constructed of wood and corrugated iron. The village presented a new, out-west appearance.

"In summer the bay was dotted with small boats. Captain Finlayson, owner of the first motor-boat in the district, was crossing and re-crossing with passengers. Many a tale could the Captain tell of his exploits in the Yellow Sea in the days when he sailed his ship to China and the Far East.

"Peter Leitch and his stalwart crew rowed the old garboard, a heavy flat-bottomed boat built for ferrying sheep and cattle. Across it were two planks upon which a motor car had to be precariously perched." Duncan Macpherson. *Gateway to Skye.*

The *Fusilier* about to leave the pier at Portree on a summer morning in the early thirties. Built in 1888, she replaced the *Glencoe* (see page 34) on the Mallaig-Kyle-Raasay run in 1931 and was herself replaced in 1934 by the *Lochnevis*. In those days steamers were built to last.

The daylight strengthens, and the sirens sound;
The last rope splashes and the engines churn;
The quayside fades. O misty isle it seems
As if no time to leave thee could be found
More fitting than the hour in which men turn
From sleeping and reluctant lose their dreams. — J F Marshall

Kyleakin. ''At Kyle Akin the late Lord Macdonald contemplated the establishment of a considerable seaport town and had imposing and splendid plans prepared for it; but the scheme proved quite abortive. The scale of houses fixed upon — two storeys with attics — was beyond the means of the people and no man of capital was got to settle in the place; and hence Kyle Akin has never attained a greater status than what about a score of respectable-looking houses can lay claim to; but it possesses a good inn. Close to the village are the ruins of an old square keep called Castle Maoil. It is said to have been built by the daughter of a Norwegian king for the purpose of levying an impost on all vessels passing the kyles excepting those of her own country.'' *Anderson's Guide to the Highlands* 1850.

The Railway Hotel, Kyle of Lochalsh. The Dingwall & Skye Railway Act was passed in July 1865 empowering the company to build 63 miles of line from Dingwall and at Kyle itself construct a station and a port. At that time Kyle was a mere village with a ferry across to Skye. It was not until November 1897 that the complete line, extended from its earlier terminus at Strome Ferry, was opened to passengers. By then the old inn had been enlarged and incomers who wanted to build houses were given land at nominal prices. As John Thomas records in *The Skye Railway*: "Kyle of Lochalsh began to look lived-in. Even property speculators tried to move in. An English gentleman offered £1000 and an annual rental of £5 for the station refreshment room. A compatriot, Dr Ogilvie of Co. Durham wanted to buy the small hotel the company had established at Kyle for conversion into a hydropathic 'for the treatment of invalids by electricity'." Steamers came and went morning and evening on the Stornoway and Portree runs and there was plenty of fishing activity. As late as 1931 the hotel remained lit by paraffin and guests went to bed with candles.

Monday September 11, 1933. The Duke and Duchess of York arriving on Skye where the Duke opened the Elgin Hostel in the grounds of Portree High School. *The Scotsman* received this photograph, the first ever from Skye on ''our new portable picture telegraph machine, the first in Britain''. According to the paper ''The weather was glorious as befitted the occasion of a Royal visit.'' Cameron of Lochiel presented local dignitaries and then the Royal party proceeded by motor car to Dunvegan Castle. ''Their route was through one of the finest scenic parts of this island of loch and mountain.''

SECTION THREE

The Heart of the Island

Portree was originally known as Kiltaraglen, taking its name from Talorgan the Culdee who had a chapel the ruins of which can still be seen near Kiltaraglen House on the road to Staffin.

When in 1540 King James V anchored his fleet in the bay, the name was, according to legend, changed to Port an Righ or the King's Harbour. Forty years later a licence was obtained from the Crown for a twice yearly market. Then the island's produce was brought in for barter — meal, butter, cheese, poultry, sheep, cattle and horses, hides, wool, linen and dried fish. In those days a cow cost 50p and a stone of cheese 5p.

In 1746 when Flora Macdonald led the fugitive Prince Charles to Portree they rested in MacNab's Inn, now the Royal Hotel. There, 27 years later, Boswell and Johnson had "a very good dinner, porter, port and punch with James Macdonald the inn-keeper who was about to emigrate". Indeed the *Nestor* lay at anchor in the bay waiting to carry Skye adventurers to the New World.

The first church in Portree was built in about 1730 and it possessed a slated roof. Boswell recorded that it had been Sir James Macdonald's intention to build a village at Portree "which would have done great good. A village is like a heart to a country. It produces a perpetual circulation and givs the country people an opportunity to make profit of eggs and many other little articles which would otherwise in good measure be lost." Before he died in Rome in 1766 Sir James had built a school in Portree but the rest of his grand plan died with him.

There was no road to Portree until 1816 when the section from Sligachan north was finished; a road from Portree to Uig was built in 1819 but it was almost a century before a road joined Portree to Staffin. When Stanhope visited Portree in 1805 he recorded that "we travel very slowly as there is no road, merely a kind of track".

"This place," said Stanhope, "will soon arrive at the dignity of a town. A jail has been recently built here but it is principally *in terrorem*, as it is always empty! There has in the memory of man, only been one felon hanged in Skye and that was for a murder sixty or seventy years ago. The gallows were pitched upon a high hill at Portree."

When the octagonal tower was built by Doctor Ban on the Meall the village was still insubstantial "little more than a score of houses, the half of them slated". A new church, now the Black Memorial Hall, had been built in 1820. At this stage Portree had a bank too and a court-room. The principal exports were cattle, sheep, wool, kelp, salted herrings, pickled salmon, dried cod and ling.

For those who believe that Portree has been overwhelmed by visitors it may be some consolation to realise that tourism is no recent phenomenon. More than 130 years ago the geological curiosities of the Storr and the Quiraing were making Portree a magnet for visitors. The Rev Thomas Grierson was on hand in 1849 to record the rush: "On the night of the 4th September, the scramble for beds in Portree was almost unprecedented. Late in the evening a coach-and-four arrived full of ladies but how or where they were lodged we could not conjecture as every corner was occupied long before their arrival; very probably they were indebted for night-quarters to the vehicle in which they had travelled. This I know, that some half-dozen gentlemen were glad to wrap themselves up in their cloaks and plaids and squat for the night on the floor of the sitting-room. There being no alternative, they wisely submitted with a good grace."

In 1860 the traveller Charles Weld found the inn excellent but was not impressed with much else: "the houses, though well-built, do not convey the idea of being occupied by a prosperous people: paneless windows are common, and the furniture of the rooms that I saw was poor and scanty." Alexander Smith was more enthusiastic a few years later: "the lower range of houses consist mainly of warehouses and fish-stores; the upper of the main hotel, the two banks, the court-house and the shops. In the bay the yacht of the tourist is continually lying and at the hotel door his dog-cart is continually departing or arriving. On the evenings of market-days farmers and cattle-dealers sit over tumblers of smoking punch and discuss noisily the prices and the qualities of stock."

The 1867 Valuation Rolls reveal that Portree was now a thriving community. It had a post office, a poor house and a woolmill. It also had a druggist, a saddler, two bakers, a steamboat agent, fish-curers, hawkers, masons, a smith, a police inspector, joiners, painters, butchers, tailors, a dressmaker and merchants of all kinds.

By the turn of the century Portree boasted a literary society, a library, a choir and a reading room but the pace was slow. "Steamers come and go, bringing mails and cargoes; carts move leisurely pierwards or countrywards to carry off these cargoes; the country-folk come into town with their shaggy ponies bearing panniers to do their shopping."

By 1906 the small metropolis had three hotels, a Territorial drill-hall and six separate churches. The Skye Gathering Hall had been built in 1878 and a guide of the times wrote of "the little fleet of fishing smacks at anchor at the quay, the nets hung up to dry with their bladder-floats and the bustle from time to time at the arrival of a steamer."

The oldest extant buildings are Portree House, and the tourist office, remarkably unchanged since William Daniell first sketched it in 1813. The meal mill at the end of Mill Road is still there but the Royal Hotel was badly damaged by fire and its appearance destroyed even more by the appalling new wing which replaced the imposing tower. The old school was torn down in 1971 and replaced by a three-storied concrete shed renowned for its ugliness. I pass it with averted eyes. Indeed, post-war building has done little to enhance the environment. Most of the old buildings in the centre of the town are "listed", a small piece of bureaucracy that seems to do nothing to protect them from the vandalism of plastic fascias and injudicious alteration.

Am Baile

Port an Righ, air a ghiorrachadh le sgioblachadh canain gu Port-righ? Neo Port Ruighe, bho fhacal nach cluinnear ro thric an diugh ag ciallachadh a' chuid iseal de shliabh monaidh neo cnuic? Se an darna fear as docha, a reir mar a tha muinntir na cearna seo dhe'n eilean 'ga fhuaimneachadh — Port-ruigheadh, le "eadh" fhollaiseach aig deireadh an fhacail.

Ach is neonach gum bheil moran de mhuinntir a' bhaile son sin a chreidsinn. Se righ as uaisle na sliabh sam bith, air cho alainn 's gum bi e, agus tha e nadurra do phriomh-bhaile a bhith an gaol air rud sam bith a chuireas ri chuid uaisleachd. Carson a bhiodh muinntir Phort-ruigheadh air chaochladh?

Mar phriomh-bhaile chan eil e ro shean; gann da cheud bliadhna. Agus tha an sluagh a' sior atharrachadh. "Co th'air fhagail de dh'fhior mhuinntir Phort-ruigheadh?" canaidh iad riut le osna is crathadh cinn. "Chan eil ach dha na tri theaghlaichean!"

Ach is neonach nach ann mar sin a bha e riamh gu ire, oir seo far an robh an Gall is an Sgitheanach ag coinneachadh o'n thoisich am baile ri fas. Luchd na croite a' sior ghluasad astigh far na duthcha anns gach ginealach, luchd dreuchd mar bhancairean is fir-lagha is maighstirean-sgoile nas dualaiche tighinn bho dheas.

Shios mu'n chladach, air an t-Sligneach neo thall air na Lotaichean, neo air arainn a' bhaile, cha robh leisg orra Gaidhlig a bhruidheann. Mar a b'fhaisg thu air Sraid Wentworth, priomh-shraid a' bhaile, b'ann a b'airde bha gleadhar na Beurla a' fas. "Cockle Street" a chanadh iad an sin ris an t-Sligneach, agus thug iad Bosville Terrace air an t-Sraid Dhubh, is iad an dul gur e adhartas a bha sin.

Ach a dh'aindeoin geasagan beaga dhe'n t-seorsa sin, is ioma fear is te a thug suil thais 'nan deidh is am bata amach a' Sgeir Mhor.

Portree harbour 1882. I am tempted by my old friend Donnie Mackenzie to risk a date for this photograph; he suggests that the paddler (moored right foreground) is the *Carham*, a small iron steamer of 179 tons gross which was bought in 1871 by the Dingwall & Skye Railway to carry passengers between the terminus at Strome Ferry and Portree. In 1880 the railway gave up its maritime activities in favour of MacBrayne although they continued the daily service to Portree until 1882. If Donnie Mackenzie is right, and he is not a man given to wild statements, here is *Carham* swinging at her anchor waiting for a purchaser. She was eventually sold to the Ramsgate Steam Ship Company and renamed *Queen of Thailand*; from then until 1886 she did a regular run between Ramsgate and French ports which came to be known as 'Shilling Emetics'.

Note the substantial private yacht moored at *Carham*'s stern, the uncompleted Quay Street, the unbuilt Marine Hotel, the thick pall of peatsmoke hanging over the village and the folly, now alas collapsed, built on The Lump by that great benefactor of Portree Alexander Macleod, An Dotair Ban. Surgeon, engineer and universal improver he was born at Kilpheadar in North Uist in 1788 and was a descendant of the Macleods of Rigg. He came to Portree about 1829 as Lord Macdonald's factor and stayed for 6 years before returning to his practice in North Uist. He returned to Portree as doctor in 1851 when he laid out the hill above Portree as a pleasure garden, planting it with flowers and shrubs. An early pioneer of tourism Dr Macleod even had bathing houses built for visitors.

This was how Portree looked when the gentlemen of the press arrived in April 1882 to cover the impending Battle of the Braes. ''Here we are, then — two Sheriffs, two Fiscals, a Captain of Police, forty-seven members of the Glasgow Police force and a number of the county constabulary'' wrote Alexander Gow of the *Dundee Advertiser* as he set off from Ross's Hotel for Balmeanach a century ago. Not surprisingly when they left Portree it was raining and it was raining when they returned with bloody noses and five prisoners.

Portree at the turn of the century. The Marine Temperance Hotel (far left) has now been built and a new row of houses added to complete Quay Street. Two steamers are moored at the pier and two large sailing vessels alongside the slip. To the left of the old gaol is the newly erected Skye Gathering Hall. "*Portree*," said David MacBrayne's guide book, "contains 2500 inhabitants, principally engaged in fishing and cloth weaving. It has four hotels, a post and telegraph office and branches of three banks. A fine view of the Storr Rocks and the Cuchullins can be got from the ruins of a small tower on a wooden eminence above the pier. Here tourists land to visit the Quiraing."

Portree from the Meall. An excellent view this of Beaumont Crescent on the shore with its 'palace' conformation — designed by Thomas Telford who also constructed the slip and the pier. The houses were built for a Captain Beaumont from stone quarried from the red cliffs of Cuddy Point.

Portree from Cuddy Point. A sailing smack at the slip, perhaps laden with a cargo of salt for curing herring. The twin jetties between which boats could be berthed and repaired at low tide can be clearly seen. Note the stakes in the foreground for drying nets.

Ten Thousand Common Soldiers

It is not surprising that so over-populated an island as Skye and one in which it was so difficult to eke out a living should have provided the greatest reservoir of manpower for the army in Britain and mercenaries in plenty for foreign powers. General Norman Macleod of Gesto had a glittering career in the Netherlands army and a grandson rose to the rank of vice-admiral in the Dutch navy; other Macleods migrated to military careers in Poland.

General Sir John Macleod of Raasay was Wellington's Director-General of Ordnance; General William MacAskill of Bracadale became Governor of Mauritius. Of General Henry Mackinnon of Skye who died in Spain while leading his men in battle Southey wrote: "Perhaps the country has never sustained so great a loss since the death of Sir Philip Sydney."

The Rev Dr Norman Macleod estimated that between 1797 and 1840 Skye made a contribution to the fighting forces of "21 lieutenant-generals and major-generals, 45 colonels, 600 commissioned officers, 10,000 common soldiers and 120 pipers". General Stewart of Garth claimed that "there are so many old soldiers settled in Skye receiving pensions for wounds and length of service that the circulation of so much money is to no small advantage to their native isle".

Once a quarter the veterans of the Peninsular wars would make their way to Portree to collect their pensions. Drams were taken and old battles refought. Portree four times a year was as busy as on a market day as the old men recalled campaigns in the Low Countries, in Spain and in India.

In former times clansmen had rallied to support their chief; in later wars it was the estate proprietor who rounded up the tenants and personally marched them towards the cannon's mouth. William Mackenzie of Trotternish wrote of Colonel Kenneth Macdonald DSO of Tote: "He recruited the Skye contingent of the Lovat Scouts and served with distinction in the South African War. He commanded the Scouts in Macedonia and at the Dardanelles. The Scouts were the last to re-embark. Colonel Macdonald takes great interest in the survivors of the men who served under him. He is a genial and affable gentleman."

Two thousand men joined up from Skye between 1914 and 1918 — one-fifth of the entire population. The war memorials in every township pay tribute to the price the island paid in both wars. Army recruiting teams still visit the island and thanks to the low job prospects and the high rate of unemployment they seldom depart without recruits.

Cnamhan Cogaidh Fad as

"Cnamhan cogaidh fad as . . .", miann a' Ghaidheil feadh ioma linn, is docha. Ag cnamhan, los gum maireadh e is nach lasadh e ro mhor is gum biodh obair ann do shaighdearan oga fad uine; fad as, eagal 's gun cuireadh e cus dragh air daoine aig an tigh! Bha rud-eigin air leth freagarrach mu'n smuain do chogaidhean beaga na h-Impireachd ri linn Bhictoria.

Bho dheireadh na h-ochdamh linn deug amach bha saighdearachd 'na ghealltanas air tomhas de chosnadh agus, mur an robh moran beairteis 'na chois, sheachnadh e co-dhiubh an dubh bhochdainn a bha cho cumanta aig baile. Ach gle thric chan ann dha'n deoin a rachadh daoine ann, gun rud-eigin 'gan taladh gu taobh. Agus gle thric b'e am breugadh gealltanas fearainn son mac a thoirt dha'n arm. Gabh Aonghas Peutan a Ra an Uige agus an litir a sgriobh e (neo, is e moran as docha, a chaidh a sgriobhadh dha) air an 8mh latha dhe'n Ghiblean, 1806:

> Unto the Hon'ble Major John Campbell, the petission of Angus Beaton Humbly Showeth
>
> That your petissioner was a Soldier in Lord Macdonald's late Regt of the Isles and Vollunteered; at the time of your petissioner's inlistment, his Father got Land and possession in Ra foresaid and is dispossessed since owing to the said Farm being Cut out in Lots; your petissioner got married since his return to the Country, and finds it very hard upon him that Himself and Father to be without Land or possession to stay in the Country after being a Soldier and a Vollunteer in his Lordship's late Regt of the Isles, Therefore
>
> May it please your Honour to consider the above Facts and see if there can be any possession granted to your petissioner and Father, and your petissioner
>
> Shall ever pray

Co-dhiubh fhuair urnuigh Aonghais Pheutain freagairt co aige tha fios, ach tha petisean neo dha dhe'n dearbh sheorsa ri'n lorg comhla ris an fhear sin ameasg phaipearan oighreachd Chlann Domhnaill. Cha robh an gealladh a bha cho cruaidh 's cho daingeann nuair a bha saighdearan oga, treuna 'gan togail is a' mairdseadh air falbh gu bragail ri cas-cheum na pioba, idir cho seasmhach nuair a thilleadh fear an sud 's fear an seo is iad loireach is leointe.

Ach feadh moran dhe'n naoidheamh linn deug lean na h-uiread dhe na Sgitheanaich ris an arm, agus an fheadhainn nach do ghabh dha'n Arm Cheangailte ghabh iad dha na Volunteers. Bha an tasdan neo dha a bha iad a' faighinn son frithealadh cola-deug de champa eacarsaich as t-samhradh na dheagh chuideachadh do ioma teaghlach. Gu dearbh, tha e air aithris mu fhear air an Taobh Sear gun robh e cho dileas dha'n Bhan-righinn is gun liostaig e ann an da mheur dhe'n t-seirbhis, an t-arm is an neibhidh, fo dhifir ainmean. Agus son a dhilseachd dhubailte fhritheil e da champa samhraidh agus, gu nadurra, choisinn e da dhuais! Bu daor an ceannach aige air sin nuair a thainig an Land League. Cha ghabhadh duine bha cho fior dhileas dha'n Chrun gnothach riutha, is ruisg iad mullach an tigh aige is loisg iad iodhlann.

Officers of the First Volunteer Battalion, Queen's Own Cameron Highlanders at their summer camp in 1891. The portly figure with the drooping moustache is the famous 'Lachie' Ross. Of him Norman Maclean recalled: "Next to the factor the most influential man in Portree was Lachlan Ross, the proprietor of the Royal Hotel. He loved to use sonorous words when he spoke English; but he could do kind and generous acts. It is strange that hotel-keepers should be invariably conservatives of the bluest dye; Lachie Ross was no exception. He was an unbending upholder of the old order. He could not think of the Island without Lord Macdonald. He had an old cannon placed on top of the brae in front of the hotel and whenever the *Lady of The Isles* came steaming round the headland of Camustianivaig Lachie Ross would fire a salute. And when the yacht passed the Black Rock he would fire another. But he had never known a day such as this when the six Braes crofters, dishevelled, hungry and soaked with rain were lodged in jail. When the crowd of villagers hissed the police,

Lachie tried to raise a cheer but not a voice joined in. The only way he found of expressing his loyalty was by providing a specially hot bath for Sheriff Ivory''.

Lachie persuaded the factor who was Captain of the local volunteers that they should turn out in a display of martial strength to deter the men of Braes from storming the jail. Notices were posted calling a full-dress parade at seven that night with their arms.

"The parade of the volunteers in Somerled Square became famous throughout the island. Not only was Lieutenant Ross very fond of using long English words, but when he got excited he mixed his native Gaelic with his acquired English with a terseness which greatly improved both languages. The company assembled, some fifty men of tried valour in kilt and hose and Lieutenant Ross gave the order which immortalised him: 'Fix beaglets and prepare for calvary!' ''

The Volunteers parade in full dress uniform in Somerled Square before embarking for South Africa and the Boer War. The corrugated iron photographic studio in front of which they posed later gave place in 1912 to the more substantial Masonic Buildings.

"H" Company of the first Volunteer Battalion of the Queen's Own Cameron Highlanders at their annual camp in Fochabers, July, 1897.

Back row left to right
Ptes A Macpherson, J Henderson, A MacLure, A MacIntosh, A MacLeod. Piper J G Mackenzie, Cpl Piper E Mackenzie (Comassie) Piper Hugh Stewart, Pte D MacLeod (Dodie) Pte John MacDonald, L/C D Macintosh, Pte John Gillies.

Centre row
Drumm J MacInnes, Cyclist K Macrae, Ptes John Mackinnon, John Beaton, Angus Nicholson, Donald Graham, Donald Dewar, Donald Kennedy, Alex M Murchison, Don Matheson, Sam Cumming, William MacLean, Ian MacConnochie

Front row
Sgt/Instructor Hamilton, Company Sergeant George Dickson, Cpl Jas Melville, Ptes Alex MacLean, Neil MacCrimmon (Solly), Don Macleod, — Macdonald, Lt James Dickson, Captain Lawrence Kane, Lt A D Mackinnon, Pte Charles MacKinnon, Pte John MacDonald, Pte William MacLeod, Sgt Angus Ross, Sgt Ron MacDonald

Sitting
Pte Don Whiteford, Pte John Sharp, Pte Dugald MacDonald, Pte Willoughby Dunn, Pte A Maclean.

Two Skyemen and two conflicting views.

"The Skye crofters have a large host of sympathising friends, but for all that, they must be sharply and sternly taught, that they cannot be allowed with impunity to disregard their country's laws by using violence or taking forcible possession of their neighbour's property. At present there does not appear to be the slightest probability that any regular employment can be found on the island for the present population." Malcolm Ferguson 1885.

"Our sympathies lie emphatically with the law-breakers. We know that this Glendale outbreak is a mere symptom of a deeply-seated social disease for which the land oligarchy and the Land Laws are answerable at the bar of eternal justice. We regard the Glendale crofters as martyrs rather than criminals — not because they are legally in the right, or because it is in any case right to break the law, but because the law is radically wrong".

Professor Blackie 1883.

An Island in Revolt

It was in Skye that the Highland battle for land reform took its most dramatic turn in the 1880's. It would be simplistic to suggest that the oppression and high handedness of landlords and their factors was the sole cause of a massive refusal to pay rents.

Overpopulation, a climate which rendered the growing of crops difficult and impossible, the failure of the herring fishings and the potato blight which led to destitution on an epic scale had over the years created a way of life which eventually became untenable even for the mildest of men.

Rack-renting and harassment encouraged many families to the ultimate solution — emigration. It was however the patent injustices of a society where a handful of proprietors had total control over the lives and destinies of whole communities which eventually led to direct action, a Royal Commission of Enquiry and the passing in 1886 of what has been described as a first instalment of justice — the Crofters' Act of 1886.

The story of the struggle for the land has been recorded vividly in James Hunter's *The Making of the Crofting Community* published in 1976 and Iain Fraser Grigor's *Mightier than a Lord* published in 1979. There is no need to rehearse the story again here. As far as Skye is concerned the campaign of protest on the Kilmuir estate, in Glendale and in the Braes was in essence a demand for the right to be given adequate land.

On the one hand there were huge tracts of uncultivated land given over to sheep or reserved for sporting purposes, on the other overcrowded townships where at best the largest patch of land was too poor to support a family. The evidence presented to the Napier Commission which toured Skye revealed a feudal state of affairs where tenants were expected to render free labour to their landlords and were, in many cases, denied the most elementary rights enjoyed by Britons in other parts of the country.

"For a parallel to this monstrous power of the landowner," wrote Alfred Russell Wallace, "under which life and property are entirely at his mercy, we must go back to medieval times or the days when, serfdom not having been abolished, the Russian noble was armed with despotic authority, while the more pitiful results of this landlord tyranny, the devastation of cultivated land, the heartless burning of houses, the reckless creation of pauperism and misery out of well-being and contentment, could only be expected under the rule of Turkish sultans or greedy and cruel pashas."

The land war lasted six years but it would be wrong to believe that the Crofters Act alleviated all the outstanding grievances. Land raids continued until the end of the century and beyond. Indeed in Skye there were raids on land belonging to the Macleod estate in 1920 while in Raasay ex-servicemen in 1921 re-occupied land from which their forebears had been removed in the 1850s.

"The circumstances under which we live here in Rona," wrote one of the land-raiders, "are the most deplorable, the place being hardly fit for goats, far less human beings, while the good land on the south end of Raasay from which we could have a decent living and for which the best of our manhood has bled and died in Flanders and elsewhere is as a sporting ground for an independent English gentleman."

Since the 1920s there has been no direct action but in recent years the islands have had more than their share of unacceptable landlordism. It manifested itself in the 1970s in the activities of the late Dr. Green on Raasay; in 1980 it was a Dutch land stripper who brought home to the people of Skye very clearly that the control of the land was completely out of their hands.

Indeed the crofter is still denied any really important say in how the natural resources around him shall be used. Pop stars and property speculators come and go. One day the land around you may be owned by a merchant banker, the next by some anonymous Swiss-based syndicate of chancers. The archaic sporting laws remain as socially divisive today as they were when they were described by a Skye crofter in 1884: "The fish that was yesterday miles away from the land was claimed by the landlord the moment it reached shore and so also were the birds of the air as soon as they flew over his land. The law made it so because landlords were themselves the lawmakers and it was a wonder that the poor man was allowed to breathe the air of heaven and drink from the mountain stream without having the factors and the whole county police pursuing him as a thief."

The battle is still not won.

Is Treasa Tuath na Tighearna

Nan gabhadh an iarmailt a mhalairt
Mar ghabhas am fearann a roinn,
Chan fhaiceamaid rionnag neo gealach
Neo tarraing ar n-anail dhe'n ghaoith

Mairi Mhor nan Oran

B'e firinn is eiginn nam faclan sin a theannaich croitearan an Eilein Sgitheanaich ri cheile 'sna bliadhnaichean o 1880 amach, gu ire nach fhacas roimhe sin neo as a dheidh. B'iad gniomhan nam bliadhnaichean sin a dhealbh clar an eilein a th'ann an diugh.

Gun teagamh, cha robh na Sgitheanaich leotha fhein 'san t-stri; o'n Bhuta Leodhasach gu Ceann Bharraidh 's o'n Pharbh gu Ceann-tire bha an tuath air lasadh an aghaidh nan uachdaran. Agus bha na sgilean poiliticeach aca a thug an argamaid gu sgairteil gu urlar Tigh nan Cumantan.

Ach bha an t-Eilean Sgitheanach aig fior chridhe na tuasaid. Tuiteamas eachdraidh a bha sin gu ire mhor. B'ann an sin a bha an fhoirneart a b'fhollaisich, bha oigridh ann nach seasadh a leithid tuilleadh, agus bha na h-iasgairean a' toirt dhachaidh eolas a Eirinn air doighean air bruidealachd nan uachdaran a cheannsachadh.

Agus gu h-araid thagh an riaghaltas an t-eilean mar raon-catha son an-fhois nan croitearan a mhuchadh mus bruchdadh e gu ar-amach — is le sin bhrosnaich iad an t-ar-amach. Rinn an Siorram Ivory grainneil air ceann a chuid pholasmain — ''an Satan 's a chuid ainglean'' — barrachd son na croitearan 's na coitearan a phutadh gu uchd catha na aon neach eile.

Gu fortanach ghleidh sliochd nan croitearan cuimhne air cliu an luchd treoireachaidh — daoine mar ''Parnell'' Stiubhart a Bhaltos, Iain Cananach an Gleanndail agus fir a' Bhraighe. Ged bu mhiann le sgoil is ughdarrasan eile na h-ainmean sin a leigeil an dearmad a chionn's gun tug iad an aghaidh air uachdranas, rinn ioma seanair is seanmhair cinnteach gun robh an euchdan air bilean an oghaichean.

Se ainmean cumhachdach a th'unnta fhathast ameasg muinntir an eilein. Chaidh gairm orra rithist anns na bliadhnaichean an deidh 1960 nuair a thug Aonadh nan Croitearan ionnsaigh air sliochd nan uachdaran air Comhairle Shiorrachd Inbhirnis, agus a chaidh aca air coignear dhe'm muinntir fhein a chur 'nan aite.

Mur a b'e na laoich a bh'ann bho chionn ceud bliadhna is neonach nach robh an dualchas Gaidhealach an diugh 'na fhaileas fann. Nuair a thionndaidh na h-uachdarain an cota, b'e sliochd na croite a ghleidh canain is dualchas. Ach gun ''Parnell'' 's a sheoid cha robh croitearan ann.

San latha th'ann tha an eachdraidh sin, a bha an imis a dhol buileach as fianuis a' mhor-shluaigh, 'ga rannsachadh 's 'ga toirt am follais na h-oigridh. Tha sin cho math, oir sluagh gun eolas air eachdraidh fhein cha shluagh idir e.

Is docha gum bheil leasanan fhathast dha na h-eileanaich anns na rinn an sinnsreachd bho chionn ceud bliadhna. Chan eil latha an uachdarain fhathast seachad anns an Eilean Sgitheanach.

Chan eil, gu fortanach, na latha a' chroiteir.

In the winter of 1880-81 the crofters of Valtos on the Kilmuir estate gave notice that they would no longer pay their extortionately increased rent. This was the first example of direct action in the war against landlordism. Their leader was John Stewart, 'the Skye Parnell'.

Gentlemen and estate workers, Waternish. In a gathering it was the tacksman and the professional classes who tended to be clean-shaven, the crofters were bearded. "Our particular set", wrote a Skye laird, "were the gentlemen farmers, parsons, doctors, retired officers. The next stratum below comprised bank managers and substantial tradesmen. They were accorded the privilege of our society but they were never invited to our houses".

Kilmuir School Treat, Duntulm, 1929.

The tall figure in the background is the naturalist, piper and author Seton Gordon who lived a large part of his life at Upper Duntulm. He wrote over two dozen books, the majority celebrating the natural delights of the island he loved more than any other. His tall kilted figure increasingly bent in his nonagenerian years was seen at every Skye Games. A member of the Scottish Pipers Association he adjudicated at the Games for many years. My last sight of him was in company with three other remarkable Skye figures at a Games held in the mid-seventies. There was himself, Dame Flora Macleod of Macleod, General Harry Macdonald of Redcliffe and his cousin Colonel 'Jock' Macdonald of Viewfield. The sum of their ages was moving towards four centuries. Gone now all of them, but memorable each in their different way to the last.

"Our education was humane, uneventful and unexciting. We scratched on slates, graduated to copy-books and were occasionally allowed the frivolity of plasticine. Each morning we recited psalms or learned the Shorter Catechism by rote, chanted arithmetical tables and erupted into the playground, scrambling for our shinty sticks as we went. As we moved to the top end of the primary school we were made aware of those patches on the world map painted red. In our final primary year we had an Empire Day lecture and we stood — whether to sing or ponder in silence, I no longer remember — in honour of the occasion". Martin Macdonald. *Jock Tamson's Bairns.*

Skye Pipe Bank marching to the Meall for the opening of Skye Week, 1950.

This was the first Skye Week ever held and it was an annual event which went on into the seventies. The initial concept was commercial — an effort to extend the short tourist season. Statistically May is one of the driest and sunniest months in the year and it was hoped that a full week of events would bring back visitors and by word of mouth increase tourism in the slack month of June. The Pipe Band played, Dame Flora held open house at Dunvegan, games were held; there were ceilidhs, exhibitions and dances.

Octogenarian Skye Crofter c 1880.

"The houses were rude but they seemed sufficiently weather-tight. Each was set down in a little oasis of cultivation, a little circle in which by labour the sour land had been coaxed into a smile of green; each small domain was enclosed by a low turfen wall and on top of one of these a wild goat-looking sheep was feeding. The land was sour and stony, the dwellings framed of the rudest materials and the people, especially the older people gave one the idea somehow of worn-out tools. In some obscure way they reminded one of bent and warped oars, battered spades, blunted pickaxes. On every figure was written hard, unremitting toil. Toil had twisted their frames, seamed and puckered their leathern faces, made their hands horny, bleached their grizzled locks. Your fancy had to run back along years and years of labour before it could arrive at the original boy or girl." Alexander Smith. *A Summer in Skye*. 1865.

Three generations.

Crofters, Fisherfield, Portree. c 1880

"They are real gentlemen in their way, with delicate inborn tact, and all the naturally courteous instincts of good breeding; and, moreover, with a keen perception of all that marks true breeding in others, as well as the pride born of self-respect. It is a hard life, of never-ending and ill-requited toil and the struggle for existence becomes harder year by year as the land becomes more improverished by the effort to yield the self same crops for generation after generation — the soil ever-deteriorating and the mouths to be fed ever increasing in number. Many a pang of hunger and cold and weariness have these men and women endured without a murmur as beseems thoroughbred Islesmen; who would have fallen low indeed in their own eyes, should they betray symptons of any such weakness". C F Gordon Cumming *In the Hebrides* 1883.

Breakish School, 1909.

Breakish school was built in the 1890s and it numbered among its distinguished pupils Donald Macmillan, the recently retired Procurator Fiscal in Skye; Lachie Mackinnon the highly respected Gaelic scholar and former Chairman of the District Council; Hume Robertson a former president of the Camanachd Association and Neil Maclean of Lower Breakish and Duncan MacRae of Upper Breakish who both rose to high office in the China Steam Navigation Company.

Since 1974 the school has been the headquarters of the West Highland Publishing Company. Where once the values and virtues of the establishment were instilled into the young, today the very fabric of the establishment is dissected and questioned by the radical *West Highland Free Press*. Yesterday education. Today re-education.

SECTION SIX

Houses and Hovels

The earliest dwellings in Skye were perched on headlands — Dunscaith, Castle Camus and Duntulm — so that the sails of an enemy could be seen coming over the horizon. In more peaceful times houses like Raasay, Flodigarry, Lyndale and Orbost were built on carefully chosen stances to command splendid views from their lawns.

In their heyday these mansions were equally splendid inside for lairds and wealthy proprietors lived in great style. Among their retinue, the Woods of Raasay, for instance, kept in Victorian times, a huge staff ranging at the top end from a chef and a tutor down to assorted scullery maids and skivvies. There was a small army to keep the grounds spotlessly maintained, a sizeable crew for their yacht — in all a staff of ninety four.

This opulence was in striking contrast to the hovels in which the majority of people lived. Due to the difficulty which many cottars had in finding land they had to site their homes on the shore and, as a witness explained to the Napier Commission, these were frequently awash: "My present house is built on the sea-shore and the tide rises to it every stormy night that comes. I have to watch and put out all my furniture, such as it is. A sister of mine was employed last winter putting out the furniture and she was sickly and died in consequence."

Others were even less fortunate. A Harlosh crofter described how at the time of the Clearances some were refused all land: "I myself saw them living under a sail, spread on three poles below high-water mark. One of the crofters — Donald Campbell — was warned by the ground officer for giving refuge to a poor man who had no house. The ground officer came and pulled down the house."

There are countless descriptions in Victorian times of the primitive nature of the typical thatched house. Some were not even built of stone. Often families evicted from a reasonable dwelling would, like aborigines, throw together some minimal form of protection. Mrs Gordon Cumming wrote in 1883 of the squalor and filth she had seen: "the huts clustering together in the middle of the sodden morass, from which are dug the damp turfs which form both walls and roof and through these the rain oozes, falling with a dull drip upon the earthen floor where the half-naked children crawl about among the puddles."

The Pennells who visited Skye after the passing of the Crofters' Act found similar distress among the poor: "The hovels were as cheerless within as without. I do not know why it is that ones takes liberties with the poor which one would not dare take with the rich. We knocked at a cottage door, one Sunday afternoon, Joseph as an excuse, asking for a light. A tall old man in his shirt-sleeves came to the door with an open Bible in his hands. Within, on the left, was the dwelling-room of the household; on the right, the stable; cattle and family share the only entrance. On the mud floor at the far end, a fire of peat burned with a dull red glow and its thick choking smoke curled in clouds about the rafters and softened the shadows. Until you see it for yourself you could not believe that in our nineteenth century men still live like this."

At this time Skye was full of visitors who could not fail to have been impressed with the gulf between the comfort of a hotel or a shooting lodge and the wretched condition of the peasantry. As the Pennells pointed out, if any of the visitors had seen such conditions in Italy "they would long since have filled columns of *The Times* with their sympathy. As it is these burdens are accepted as a matter of course, or sometimes even as but one of the many picturesque elements of Highland life. From one writer one hears of the Skye lassies, half hidden under bundles of heather, stopping to laugh and chatter. We saw no smiles, no signs of contentment. An Englishman who last summer spent a week in Skye has since told us how day after day he and his wife went upon their excursion lunchless, because in the first village to which they came they emptied their luncheon-basket among the half-naked, half-starved children they found there."

The hovels of the poor were smoky, insanitary, lacking in every convenience but as Sheriff Nicolson said, by some miracle of resilience:

> *Many a poor, black cottage is there*
> *Grimy with peat smoke;*
> *Sending forth in the quiet evening air*
> *Purest of incense.*
> *Reared in those dwellings have brave ones been;*
> *Brave ones are still there.*
> *Forth from their darkness on Sunday I've seen*
> *Coming pure linen,*
> *And, like the linen, the souls were clean*
> *Of them that wore it.*

Snighe-dubh agus Bochdainn

Do mhoran an diugh tha an seann tigh-tughaidh 'na sheorsa de shuaicheantas air saoghal neo-chiontach a dh'fhalbh — "mo dhachaidh bheag fhein" le ballachan geal le aol, tughadh grinn agus ceo na mona ag eirigh gu socair an ciaradh feasgair ciuin. Tha luchd-turuis agus an treas ginealach de shliochd nan Gaidheal 'sna bailtean mora gu h-araid buailteach dha'n bhruadar sin.

Ach is neonach gur ann mar sin a bha. Tha gach fianuis a th'againn, bho sgriobhadh nan Gall beairteach a bhiodh ag cuairtearachd mu thuath anns an naoidheamh linn deug agus bho shuil a' chamara, ag cur an ceill dhuinn dealbh a tha gu dubh air a chaochladh. Bochdainn, salachar is easlaint as motha a tha ri'm faicinn innte; an t-urlar fo dhoimhneachd innearach an ceann shios an tighe agus na ballachan a' sruthadh le snighe-dubh 'sa cheann shuas. Agus leis mar a bha iad air an sgreamhachadh leis an t-sealladh sin is gann a bha na Goill a' faicinn nan daoine idir, ach mar seorsa de dheircich a bu ghann a bhoineadh dha'n chinne-daonna.

Agus am b'ann mar sin a bha? Is neonach gur ann buileach. Gun teagamh bha bochdainn is salachar is easlaint ann, ciamar nach biodh. Ach a chionn's nach robh doigh air an seachnadh cha b'iad sin na nithean a mhair an cuimhne nan daoine a chaidh an togail unnta.

Dhaibh-san b'e dachaidhean a bh'unnta, truagh's gun robh iad. Aitichean far an robh carthannas is ceilidh ag cumail tomhas de smachd air bochdainn, aitichean tearainnte far am faodadh iad magadh air a' bhumailear Ghallda a' didearachd aig an dorus ann an canain nach tuigeadh e. Thuig an Siorram

MacNeacail, Gaidheal bho thaobh nan uachdaran, gum faodadh an t-anart agus an t-anam a thigeadh amach air dorus an tigh-tughaidh a bhith a cheart cho glan ri dad a nochd thar stairsnich an tighe mhoir.

Agus a thaobh an tighe mhoir fhein b'ann ainneamh a chunnaic a' mhor-chuid de Sgitheanaich e ach bho shealladh a' sgalaig neo an t-searbhanta. Chan ann air do ghluinean a' sguradh leac an teinntein neo ag criomadh nan cnamh comhla ris na coin aig an dorus chuil as fhearr a ni ailleachd sheomraichean farsaing agus chuirtearan mheilbheid druidheadh ort.

Gun teagamh, bha cobhair anns an tigh mhor do chuid a bha teicheadh bho shaoghal an t-snighe-dhubh is an urlair chreadha. Ma bha aite mar bhan-altruim neo bean-tighe ag iarraidh tomhas de dh'irisleachd eadar iseal is uasal a bhiodh air a mheas mi-chneasda an diugh, cha b'ann mar sin a bhathas 'ga fhaicinn le moran ann an linn Bhictoria.

Ach bha a' bhearn eadar bothan tughaidh ag crubadh an cois a' chladaich agus tigh mor na pairce reidh air an rudha cho mor is nach robh doigh a mhaireadh e taobh astigh criochan aon eilein. Bhuail dudach a' Land League air monaidhean Ghleanndail agus beanntan Throndairnis a' cheud bhuille anns a' ghluasad a thoisich air na ballachan aig an da chuid a chrithneachadh.

An diugh tha an tigh tughaidh is an tigh mor nas cothromaich na bha iad. Tha iad le cheile dualach a bhith 'nan tobhtaichean loma, a' sior chrionadh gu lar.

Na deanamaid cus caoidh air sgath sin.

Talisker House. ". . . the court before the house is most injudiciously paved with round bluish-grey pebbles which are found upon the seashore, so that you walk upon cannon-bullets driven into the ground," observed Boswell on September 23, 1773. The court is still so paved.

Scorribreac Lodge, Portree. In Victorian and Edwardian times it was the winter seat of Lady Macdonald of the Isles. "Her husband was a permanent invalid; her son Archibald had been killed in the Boer War and her son Godfrey was married in 1908. Armadale Castle, the Regency Gothic mansion in the South of Skye was becoming too large and expensive for residence by Lady Macdonald and her daughter the Hon Iona. The Lodge was a dower house from which she could overlook and stimulate the activities of Portree with the benevolent rule that keeps a community lively, even though it sometimes exasperates individuals. She instituted an annual flower-show with prizes; she gave treats to the school children and suggested the plan of weekly club meetings for the country students who were in lodgings." Isobel Macdonald *A family in Skye. 1908-16.*

The lodge was converted into a hotel after the last war and renamed the Coolin Hills.

Waternish House in its heyday. Now alas a ruin. Its most noted owner was Captain Macdonald, a remarkable naturalist who tamed both seals and otters and treated them like household pets when he wasn't shooting them. "Captain Macdonald's pet otters generally roll upon some nice green turf between leaving the water and entering the house. The otters which Captain Macdonald meets with in North Uist are lighter in colour than those which he kills in Skye; a fact which he accounts for by the consideration that the former live principally in fresh water while our Skye otters frequent the sea almost exclusively. The largest dog otter that Captain Macdonald has killed in Skye weighed 27lbs and he considers 22lbs a good weight. I have been amused to see one of Captain Macdonald's present otters toying with a small eel, tossing it into the water and retrieving it again and again before eating it." H A Macpherson *A Fauna of the North West Highlands and Skye*.

    "You will be *shocked* to hear that I got seven Peregrines here from the middle of April to the middle of May, so I have got no nests on my ground this year, but there must be one about Dunvegan Head, for as I was driving down to Ardmore last week I met one of my shepherds who attends to the traps and who told me that a few minutes before he had seen a Peregrine which was pursued by two lapwings, evidently in defence of their young; but Mr Falcon soon turned the tables and swooping down clutched one of them carrying it off towards Dunvegan Head". Captain Macdonald, July 1889. In spring of 1891 Captain Macdonald killed six adult peregrines at Waternish. This Victorian zest for destruction accounts for the present lacuna in Hebridean wildlife. But the captain was not all bad. He took two eaglets from a nest at Dunvegan Head and they "became his familiar companions, descending from a great elevation to join him on his walks, answering his whistle and retrieving the game he shot for their own larder."

Above. Armadale Castle. Architect James Gillespie Graham, 1815. Once the interior was richly vaulted, now it lies unroofed. *Below*. Raasay House one of the most architecturally interesting buildings in the Hebrides. A laird's house, then a sporting mansion, later a hotel, now HQ of an adventure school.

Hovels, Bayfield, Portree. "I have seen a good deal of scrofulous disease, a good deal of lung disease and a large proportion of eye disease, due to the houses, feeding and want of clothing. I think the diet of the people much too limited, even in a good year — potatoes, fish and meal". Dr Fraser of Edinbane, 1883.

"To speak of comfort is a mockery. All the cottages we went into were alike in their poverty and darkness. As a rule the fire burned in the centre on a circle of stones and over it from the roof, hung chain and hook for the kettle. They have not changed one jot or tittle since a century ago, they moved Pennant to pity". Joseph and Elizabeth Pennell 1888.

Monkstadt House which takes its name from the cell of monks who established themselves on the island in nearby Loch Chaluim Chille. Legend relates that an infant son of the Chief of the Macdonalds fell from a window of Duntulm castle and was dashed to death on the rocks below. That, combined with the depressingly frequent manifestations of the spectral ghost of Donald Gorm persuaded the Chief, Donald Gorm Og to build himself a new house 5 miles away along the coast. Building began in 1732 and Monkstadt may well have been the first house to have a slated roof in Skye — Duntulm was thatched. Sir Alexander farmed extensively in this fertile area and employed in addition to his household staff, gardeners, a grieve, a blacksmith, a cooper, a tailor, grooms, salmon fishers, herdsmen and all the skilled men necessary to sustain an eighteenth century rural community. Here the brilliant James Macdonald, known as 'the Scottish Marcellus' was born on Boxing Day 1741. On Sunday June 29 1746 Prince Charles and Flora Macdonald landed on the shores of Monkstadt after their flight from the Outer Isles. Monkstadt was finally deserted by the Macdonalds in 1789 — it was then that Alexander Wentworth, second Lord Macdonald decided to re-establish the family seat in Armadale. Some years ago the roof was removed and the house has fallen into progressive decay. In December, 1982 the *Free Press* revealed that a new owner of Monkstadt had drawn up plans to restore what had become a mere shell. The work is expected to take ten years to complete.

The Post Office, Earlish, two miles south of Uig, at the turn of the century.

Gesto House in 1891. Here it is seen in its heyday when it had gardens with formal walks and the upstairs drawing room was decorated in the Japanese style. The exterior walls were covered with flowering creepers, roses and honeysuckle. This picture was taken by Jessie Hall Scott who kept house for her brother Adam Scott. The family originally from Roxburghshire had occupied the house for three generations.

David Roberts of Orbost suggests that the original house may have been built in the 1760s.

The Macleods of Gesto were the oldest cadet family of the Macleods of Harris and Dunvegan and their ownership of the lands of Gesto may well date to 1425. In 1825 the MacLeod chief refused to renew Captain Neil Macleod's tack and to prevent any of the family using the name 'Gesto' in future, the farms of Drynoch, Summardale and Gesto were made into one great sheep walk, 1500 souls being dispossessed in the process.

The lease of Drynoch with Gesto went to the Scotts and by 1851 John Scott was living at Gesto as a store farmer of 20,000 acres employing 24 servants and labourers. At the time of this photograph Jessie and her sister Christabel were living at Gesto with a house servant, cook, coachman, gardener, farm servant and shepherd. Unroofed and ruined the house has recently been bought by a descendant of the Scotts and he has tentative plans to restore it. David Roberts writes: ''Gesto typifies the ambitions of the Skye tacksman in domestic building. As built, Gesto had two main rooms on the ground floor, a kitchen with an ill-lit pantry and store separated by the lobby and stair from another low room perhaps used as a dairy and dining hall for farm servants. Above the dining hall was the drawing room with a bedroom and closet above the kitchen and pantry''. There were subsequent additions including a kitchen, a dairy and a boxlike porch. ''The site of Gesto is superb. The house has its feet almost on the sea-shore of the sheltered inlet. On the headland away from the house is a heronry and a large neatly kept and white-washed steading complex. As though to underline the isolation of most Skye houses from a road network there is a fine boathouse lofted over. The building with its wide elliptical archway is a short walk from the house and it must have been much easier to travel loch and sea than the boggy heights above the house. No doubt the decision to unroof Gesto was taken to escape the burden of taxation; the building salvage of wood and slates also had considerable value . . . ruin becomes more apparent with every hard winter that passes.''

Some of the Gesto staff. Although the house itself was relatively small the farmland attached to it was considerable and it needed plenty of labour. Gesto was a large tack which was divided into five 'hirsels' after the clearances. The servants here, are seen in their working clothes not the Sunday best they would have donned for the travelling photographer. Jessie Scott who took the picture in 1891 had given up watercolours to concentrate on the exciting prospects of photography.

Orbost House. Kenneth Robertson-Macleod of Orbost with his wife Isabella, seated left on an impossibly Jacobean chair amidst a bevy of daughters with one suitor, Mr Macdonald of Waternish. Alexander Smith, was Isabella's brother-in-law; he described the estate of Orbost as his favourite choice of a place to live — " . . . the house itself is the only thing that can reasonably be objected to, it is one of those elegant, expressionless houses in the Italian style, too modern, and villa like; it has not taken to the island, the island has not taken to it."

Of the daughters most made "fortunate" marriages, becoming Lady Bullough of Rum, Mrs Macdonald of Kingsburgh, Mrs Hilleary of Tayinloan and Lady Tarn. Beatrice, standing left of the door, married late in life and eventually ran Orbost as a none too successful hotel.

The splendour of the Georgian and Regency house is now secured thanks to superb restoration by the architectural historian and present owner Dr David Roberts. The heavy railings in the photograph have disappeared. Cast iron replacements have been delivered but are not yet in place.

Sir William Tarn's daughter, Otta Swire recalled in her *Skye, The Island and its Legends* that Orbost was one of the few great houses in Skye where the peacocks and peahens which walked the lawns so elegantly actually ended their lives on the dining room table. Orbost, recalled Otta Swire, has a ghost which has kept up with changing technology. " . . . the ghost of a coach and six which is heard but not seen. It drives up to the front door not infrequently with considerable noise and rattle and clamping of bits, stamping of hoofs. Of late, however it has been mechanised, which is most upsetting. Now it is a powerful car or lorry which drives up: the brakes are applied, later the clutch is let in and gears and acceleration can be heard as it departs".

SECTION SEVEN

The Sporting Scene

When it was discovered that there was a vast playground in the Highlands from which most of the population had been transported; that it was teeming with fish and game, and that there was still a reservoir of cheap and subservient labour to make a sportsman's stay comfortable, then the wealthy descended on it with cries of delight. Islands round Skye like Raasay and Rum were given over exclusively to sport and the interests of those who came to shoot and stalk.

Unfortunately there is a traditional conflict between farming and the pursuit of game. In Raasay the Woods introduced, for the delectation of their guests, a plague of rabbits. It was estimated by a witness appearing before the Napier Commission that in the 1880s there were 30,000 of them on the island eating for dear life: "If we allow that seven rabbits eat as much grass as one sheep, then we have a stock equal to more than four thousand sheep which would be enough for the whole island of Raasay to support."

Shootings in Skye formed a useful addition to an estate's income but the crofters were regarded as a nuisance and were kept firmly underfoot. "I believe," said another Napier witness, "dogs are not allowed, except in a few instances; and if a cat should venture outside a door, a gamekeeper is watching with poison, traps or gun to destroy it."

The presence on good shooting ground of what one sporting writer described as "an ignorant lot of creatures" rendered Skye less attractive than stable parts of Scotland like Perthshire: "The poor-rates at the best of times are out of all proportion", wrote the property correspondent of *The Times*, "to those in the mainland parishes; while in the worst seasons the purchasers will have the privilege of accumulating hopeless arrears of rent and feeding a population of starving paupers, who may abuse him for a tyrant when the pressure has gone by."

In any case Skye, for stalking or grouse was not considered a good bargain: "Lord Macdonald has devoted large ranges of his country to deer, they do not take kindly to the soil or climate. The heads are by no means fine and the harts are far from heavy."

When the government sent gunboats to Skye to bring the crofters to heel, many shootings remained unlet. "I believe," wrote a visitor, "owing to the crofters' ill-advised squabbles with their landlords, parties in the south did not care to venture amongst them. I know from personal knowledge that not a few parties in London had written to friends asking them if they thought it would be safe to visit Skye this summer."

Maor is Lann

Is fheudar gur ann air linn an aigh air choireigin a bha Niall MacLeoid a' smaoineachadh nuair a thainig na briathran bho pheann ainmeil:

O cait bheil na gaisgich a dh'araich do ghlacan
Bu shuilbhire macnas mu stacan a' cheo?
Le fudar 'ga sgailceadh bho'n cuilbheirean glana,
Is na mial-choin 'nan deannaibh nach fannaich 'san toir.

Mu'n am 'san robh esan beo, 'san darna leth dhe'n naoidheamh linn deug, bha an t-am sin fada seachad — ma bha e riamh ann!

Is neonach nach eil e nas fhaisge air an fhirinn a dh'fhiosraich e 'na linn fhein nuair a tha e a' toirt tarraing air ''maor is lann air gach alltan agus ob'' ann am bardachd eile. Fiu's na bu traithe 'san naoidheamh linn deug na MacLeoid bha Tormod Og Sgoirebreac a' maoidheadh air mar a bha uachdarain an latha ag cuingleachadh a chead seilg: ''Cul mo laimhe do laghan fiar, a tha toirmeasg biadh thug Dia dha'n duine!''

Ach a dh'aindeoin innleachdas bhard is docha gum biodh e cho math aideachadh nach robh an t-Eilean Sgitheanach riamh air na fior bharrachan nuair a thigeadh e gu sealg. Bha frith aig a' Mhorair Dhomhnallach, gun teagamh, air arainn a' Chuilthinn, agus bu daor an ceannach air sin a bh'aig na croitearan a chaidh a sgiursadh sios an cois na mara a dh'fhagail feurach aig na feidh. Ach bu shuarach an t-sealg a bha ri lorg ann, agur air mointichean loma fior mheadhoin an eilein, an taca ri frithean ainmeil tir-moir.

Chan e gun do chuir sin casg air na h-uachdarain is an fheadhainn a bhiodh air aoigheachd aca. Rinn iad a' chuid a b'fhearr dhe na bh'ann. Agus mur an robh an t-eilean riamh ro ainmeil a thaobh a chuid feidh neo a chearcan-fraoich, bha co-dhiubh am bradan ri lorg ann, agus corr lochan dubh anns a' mhonadh far an toilleadh am breac is an caimeineach

An diugh chan eil moran sealg is fhiach ainmeachadh 'san eilean, ach iasgach nan aibhnichean. A reir na h-uachdarain aig am bheil na coirichean orra tha iad air an dubh chlaoidh le poidsearan! Feumar aideachadh nach eil an t-Eilean Sgitheanach ach mar an corr dhe'n Ghaidhealtachd nuair e thig e gu poidseadh; dha'n mhor-chuid chan e gnothach gun chliu a th'ann idir breac a thoirt a linne.

An robh e air a chaochladh anns an linn a dh'fhalbh? Is neonach sin, a dh'aindeoin uachdranas chruaidh agus peanasachadh an-iochdmhor. Tha e duilich a chreidsinn gun robh am maor riamh cho eifeachdach 's a dhuraigeadh a mhaighstir.

Captain Macdonald's tame hind, Waternish. Fallow deer were introduced into Skye by the Captain, they were not indigenous. Captain Macdonald recalled in 1888 that as a boy forty years earlier he had been "shown the remains of stone traps or enclosures which, he opines, must now be overgrown with moss and heather. On the 8th July 1888 the Captain told me that these enclosures or traps (built of stone) narrowed gradually until the animal was fairly hemmed in". "In the seventies and eighties of the nineteenth century", wrote Canon Macleod of Macleod in 1920, "as times grew worse both the Castle and the Ullinish shootings were let. I find about 1885 shooting rents of £1100. This seems a very substantial sum but very large reductions have to be made. Shooting lodges have to be built, kept in repair and furnished. The wages of keepers have to be paid and dwelling-houses provided for them; rates and taxes have to be paid on the rents. I see signs that this door is closing. The crofters are beginning to keep guns and use them and even if they do not poach, the number of dogs they keep must be very harmful to game."

Sportsman and his life support. This splendidly frozen still-life of ponies, dogs and ghillies was taken probably in the early 1920s or perhaps just before the Great War. "The ponies of Skye were sold at four annual fairs held at Portree between May and November. When I was a boy I eagerly looked forward to those markets. At a September market a neighbouring large farmer exposed for sale a number of fillies ranging in age from three to five years. None of those animals had ever had a human hand upon her and none had ever been under a roof. They were guided by an old led horse to whom they clung closely in their nervousness and they were all strong, powerful animals. With their flowing manes and tails they seemed to my untrained eye to be perfect pictures." John Macdonald. *Highland Ponies*.

A ten-point stag shot at the head of Loch Ainort, September 1933. From left to right: Dugald Macdonald, under-keeper; Harry Macleod; Alec Fraser, and William Fraser, head-keeper on Lord Macdonald's Sconser deer forest.

Fox hunters, Waternish estate.

"In the year 1764 the Gentlemen in Skye, for the first time entered into a resolution to diminish the number of foxes and for this purpose offered a premium of three shillings for each fox that was destroyed; in consequence of this offer no less than one hundred and twelve foxes were killed in the year 1765 in the single district of Trotterness. To diminish the number and even to exterminate the foxes is a matter of importance to all inhabitants." John Walker. 1808.

"I remember finding a den high up in the Coolins about the beginning of July after the cubs had been removed. My attention was attracted by the smell and when I inspected the remnants of the carcases I counted eight black-faced lambs' heads, dozens of grouse, ptarmigan, rabbits, hares, rats, mice and frogs. All this was within sight and it would be difficult to say how much more was inside the den." John Macdonald, 1937.

SECTION EIGHT

The Quality at Leisure

There were two worlds in Skye in the nineteenth century; the world of plenty and the world of want. At the top of the scale were men like Sir Donald Currie, founder and Chairman of the Union Castle line, tenant of the island of Scalpay, north of Broadford. His yacht *Iolaire*, in reality a small liner, was attended by a steam-launch to take guests ashore for picnics.

In the summer the Macleod of Macleod took up residence in Dunvegan and Sir Alexander and Lady Alice Bosville Macdonald of the Isles sped north from their Yorkshire estates to receive the fealty of their people at Duntulm. It was all delightfully feudal in those long Edwardian days of summer. "Good service was asked for," recalled Lady Alice in 1929, "and given, but the servant was absolutely confident that his master would care for his welfare and defend him in sickness or any misfortune."

When the Skye Balls held in the Gathering Hall every September were over the quality, like swallows, departed for warmer climes leaving the peasantry to the long cold winter. "Her Ladyship," wrote Elizabeth Macdonald the factor's wife in 1912, "reminds me of a certain nobleman in the Bible who gathered his servants together and said 'occupy yourselves till I come', and then straight way took his departure. She has given us all our work to do and then on Tuesday off she goes to London for the winter, and woe betide that wicked and slothful servant who has not made good use of his talents when she returns. The Viewfield and Redcliffe families are going off too, the work is left to a few of us, none with much leisure. But she is a wonderful woman,

so clever, and so kind and good too." The 'wonderful woman' was the other Lady Macdonald of Sleat a great organiser of good works for the poor.

There were still plenty of hands to fetch and carry and in the big mansions the days passed quickly in sport and pleasure. "One would fancy from the richness of the carpets, beauty of decoration and perfection of cuisine," wrote a visitor to Duisdale House, "that one had been transported to London instead of being in the wilds of Skye."

Duisdale is now a hotel, Kinloch too and Skeabost House, Flodigarry, Greshornish, Duntulm, Portree House and many another.

Income tax and death duties were a great leveller. The Rev Norman Maclean, former chaplain to King George V who married Lord Macdonald's daughter, the Honourable Iona, described how sad his mother-in-law seemed when all the wealth vanished: "Long gone were the days when *The Lady of The Isles* waited at the wooden pier of Stromeferry for the special train coming along the curved shores of Lochcarron; the days of horses and chariots and of Armadale Castle full of guests; gone the joyous days at Cowes and the evenings at the Royal Yacht Club and dinners with the Prince of Wales; gone her gallant sons, leaving her house empty and desolate. There she sat with bandaged eyes, bent but with her will unbroken, facing the future with unabated courage. With her the feudal age ended in our island. She was in very truth *ultima Romanorum*."

Na Cinn-feadhna aig Baile

B'ann aig deireadh na seachdamh linn deug a chuir An Clarsair Dall a bhardachd ainmeil ri cheile, ag caoidh mar a bha na fasain Ghallda ag ealadh air Dun-bheagain nuair a ghabh Ruairidh Og an oighreachd os laimh an deidh bas athair, Iain Breac MacLeoid.

Chaidh a' chuibhle mu'n cuairt,
    Grad thionndaidh gu fuachd am blas;
Do chunnacas fein uair
    Dun ratha nam buadh seo thraigh;
Gheibhte ann tathaich gach duain,
    Is iomadh mathas gun chruas gun chas;
Dh'fhalbh an latha sin uainn,
    Is tha na tighean gu fuaraidh fas.

Nam bu bheo e da cheud bliadhna as deidh sin nach ann aige a bha am fior aobhar caoidh!

Aig deireadh na naoidheamh linn deug bha a' chuibhle air lan char a chur dhith agus bha am fuachd 'na rag reothadh. Bha an fheadhainn a thill dhachaidh gu na caistealan is na loidsichean aig deireadh an t-samhraidh cho Gallda ri duine riamh a chluich air raointean Eton; cha robh Gaidhealach ach an t-ainm, agus cha chainnte fiu's sin ach mu chuid dhiubh.

Gu dearbha, cha b'ann dhachaidh a bha a' mhor-chuid dhiubh tilleadh ach dha'n tighean-samhraidh; bha na dachaidhean mu dheas, gle thric an Lunnainn, agus cha robh rompa mu thuath ach spors is saorsa agus a dheanamh cinnteach gun robh na h-oighreachdan aca 'gam frithealadh gu doigheil leis na sgalagan ris na dh'fhag iad an urra iad.

Gun teagamh, is docha nach b'ann buileach mar sin a bha na dearbh sgalagan — bho'n bhaillidh gu sguidilearan a' chidsin — ag coimhead air a' chuis. Chumadh iadsan amach gun robh obair is cosnadh an cois imrich an t-samhraidh seo. Is mor na dh'fhuilingeas daoine aig nach eil roghainn cosnaidh ach roghainn na h-eiginn.

Ach dh'fhalbh an latha sin, cuideachd, uainn. Thug a' Cheud Chogadh Mor buille bhais dha, is chur caran na cuibhle as deidh an Darna Cogadh as dha buileach glan.

Agus na tighean? Tha cuid dhiubh, gun teagamh, gu fuaraidh fas; agus a' chuid nach eil tha iad an diugh 'nan tighean-osda do dh'aoighean nach eil dad nas Gallda na an fheadhain le ainm Gaidhealach a bhiodh ag gabhail a' chuairt shamhraidh ud bho chionn suas ri ceud bliadhna.

The Waternish family. A black man, some say an Australian aborigine, was part of the retinue; did he live in the grass hut?

The Woods having a picnic, Raasay. Edward Herbert Wood of Sudbourne Hall, Suffolk bought the island of Raasay in 1876. A plutocratic product of the Potteries he had vast quantities of cash and a thirst for a Highland sporting estate. His interests and that of his family were constantly at conflict with the people.

"I am now Free Church minister of Raasay for nearly sixteen years. A medical man who spent a couple of years on the island said 'the prevailing disease is poverty and the chief remedy is food'. The greatest grievance is the loss by game. Game is the first and principal consideration. This being the case, however kindly Mr Wood is disposed to be, yet the crofters must suffer serious loss. I admit that proprietors who have means and inclination are entitled to a reasonable amount of sport but I do not think it a kind treatment of his tenants that he should reserve the best of his land exclusively for sporting purposes and leave the people to continue delving miserable patches." — Statement to the Napier Commission, 1884. Mr Wood died in 1886 but his widow and daughters continued to dominate the island until it was sold in 1912 to Baird the iron founders.

Picnic at Waternish. There was an unbridgeable gulf between the standard of living of those who owned houses like Waternish, Orbost, Gesto, Kingsburgh, Skeabost and those who waited upon them, fetching and carrying for long hours at wages so low that they offended against even the most minimal standards of decency.

Only at Dunvegan Castle, Raasay House and here at Armadale did this degree of opulence obtain in Victorian Skye. It was conspicuous extravagance amidst distressingly conspicuous deprivation. This insulated world of comfort and luxury with the steam yacht anchored in the bay was not to last beyond the Great War.

Family at Husabost. By far the most famous son of Husabost was Alexander Nicolson. The future sheriff was born here in 1827 and like all the children of the big Skye houses he was educated by a tutor and prepared for university. At Edinburgh Nicolson gained high honours in literature and philosophy and intended to qualify for the Free Church ministry. He soon discovered, as he put it, 'the officer's uniform in that excellent body is painfully tight'. Journalist, law officer, advocate this 'big boned Celt with a look of strength, and kindliness in his large and strongly marked features' became Sheriff-Substitute of Kirkcudbright in 1872 and was appointed a member of the Napier Commission in 1883. Nicolson was a great Cuillin climber and was the first to gain the highest point in 1873 — the peak be conquered, Sgurr Alasdair, is named after him. He was a lyric writer of some charm and his most widely quoted lines were written in the Sligachan Visitors' Book: "Jerusalem, Athens and Rome, I would see them before I die: But I'd rather not see any one of these three Than be exiled for ever from Skye." Nicolson died in 1893.

Family group at Armadale Castle. King Edward VII who commands the scene was a yachting crony of Lord and Lady Macdonald. He came to Skye in 1902 to open Uig pier and took the opportunity to honour Armadale with his presence.

The Inn, Isle Ornsay. Opening Day 1888. Standing in the doorway is the kenspeckled inn-keeper ''Eirdsi Mor'' Nicolson with his two sisters. Oral tradition suggests that the sailor with the pipe on the right of the group is averting his face from the camera to conceal a missing eye. Is the gentleman with the stick one of the Macdonalds of Armadale Castle?

Somerled James Brudenell Macdonald (1849-1874). The photograph of Somerled and his pony 'Jacky' was taken in January 1855 when the lad was six. He was the son of Godfrey William Wentworth, the fourth Lord Macdonald who lived extravagantly and finding himself deeply in debt was forced in 1847 to sell portions of the family inheritance including the whole of North Uist and Kilmuir in Skye. On the death of his father in 1863 Somerled became chief but he died at the early age of 25.

On the occasion of his coming of age in 1930, Alexander Godfrey, the future Lord Macdonald receives from the tenantry at the ancestral seat of Armadale a matched pair of sporting guns. The castle was still inhabited by the family and their estates extended to 41,700 acres.

Norman Macleod, the 26th Chief, was born in 1839. Over the years both the Macleod and Macdonald families have married English wives and educated themselves at English schools — their detribalisation is complete. The last Macleod to speak Gaelic was Emily the sister of the 25th Chief who died in 1896. John Macleod the 29th Chief (b. 1935), Lord Godfrey Macdonald (b. 1947) Chief of the Clan Donald and Sir Ian Macdonald, (b. 1947) 25th Chief of Sleat are all Eton-educated English-speaking monoglots.